Unread

Unread

A Memoir *of* Learning (*and Loving*) *to* Read *on* TikTok

OLIVER JAMES
with M. P. HENRY

UNION
SQUARE
& CO.
NEW YORK

The author and editor have made every effort to reproduce the substance of the conversations relied on in this book, but some have been edited and condensed for clarity and space. Some names and identifying details have been changed.

Any trademarks, names, logos, and designs are the property of their owners. Unless specifically identified as such, use herein of any third-party trademarks, company names, or celebrity or personal names, likenesses, images, or quotations, does not indicate any relationship, sponsorship, or endorsement between the author, the publisher, and the trademark owner, company, celebrity, or person.

Cover design by Patrick Sullivan
Cover art by Shutterstock.com: Joern (book),
Odam Asdi Artosa (phone UI), Microstock Yucred (Icons)

Union Square & Co.
Hachette Book Group
1290 Avenue of the Americas, New York, NY 10104
unionsquareandco.com
@unionsqandco

First Edition: February 2026

Union Square & Co. is an imprint of Grand Central Publishing, a division of Hachette Book Group, Inc. The Union Square & Co. name and logo are registered trademarks of Hachette Book Group, Inc.

Print book interior design by Rich Hazelton

Library of Congress Cataloging-in-Publication Data has been applied for.

ISBNs: 978-1-4549-5940-3 (hardcover); ISBN 978-1-4549-5941-0 (ebook)

Printed in Canada

MRQ-T

10 9 8 7 6 5 4 3 2 1

To people like me:
misjudged, labeled, and forgotten about.

I see you.

"Reading is to the mind what exercise is to the body."

—Joseph Addison

CONTENTS

PROLOGUE

Right up to the last second, I didn't know if I was really going to do it. Say the five words that would come to change my life. It was such an embarrassing thing to admit.

It was 2021 and my TikTok account already had a large following. A lot of strangers to tell my biggest secret to. I wasn't sure if this was better or worse than the people who *actually* knew me finding out. But I guess that's part of the reason I wanted to tell my followers: to have someone—a lot of someones—to be accountable to. I'd been a personal trainer for years by then. I knew that one of the things that helps people reach their fitness goals isn't only what the trainer teaches you, but the fact that there's someone else there, waiting on you to show up to the gym. Someone to help mark your progress, provide guidance along the way if you don't know your next step, encourage you when you feel like quitting.

If I told everyone, there would be thousands of people out there who would know I was on this mission. Thousands of people to mess up in front of. Or thousands of people to grow in front of. Scary.

Failure would be hard enough with people watching, but to me, it would be a whole lot worse to give up trying in front of a huge virtual audience. Giving up wasn't an option.

So I was going to tell everyone. It was a matter of . . . well, I guess just *doing* it. I sat in my car with the windows up even though it was hot. This required privacy and concentration. Heart beating out of my chest, I set my phone up on the dash like I had done a million times before, took a deep breath to steady myself, and nearly threw up.

For thirty-two years I had been hiding my secret in shame and embarrassment; a whole lot of people out there didn't know, and they never would if I didn't tell them. Did I want to blow it up now?

Yes.

Because living a lie is exhausting. Especially when the lie keeps you in a place where you can't understand the world the way everyone else does. When it can literally mean the difference between life and death, because you can't read a simple warning label on a bottle or a detour sign on the road.

By then I knew I had OCD, ADHD, dyslexia, and anxiety. All three were triggered right then.

I pressed the red record button, the timer started ticking, and I looked at myself on the screen and said, to me and everyone else, the five magic words.

"What's up? I can't read."

As a kid, when I first tried learning to read, it went like this: Say I was in a classroom and I was the first kid in the second row and the first row had four kids. Now the teacher would have the first kid in the first row read the first two lines. I thought cool, I'll follow along and pick out the words, kind of like when you decipher a code, or an algebra problem, by figuring out what the symbols meant.

Second kid, third kid, fourth kid, same story. Meanwhile I'd also count the lines so I knew where mine was, so I could figure out any of the same words in my part. So I was "reading" the words as symbols, instead of learning the letter sounds and context well enough to use broadly. It worked well enough to pass but not well enough to really *read.* I would practice my lines before they would ask me to read. Remember cartoons that would have a bouncing ball over song words for kids to sing along? That's basically what I was doing. I would watch the words that they were reading, and when the kid would say the word, I'd remember or write down that word and memorize it. Most of the time I could fill in the words I didn't know by putting in what made sense.

Now, fast forward. As I got older I had learned a few words at a time I needed to know them in order to text, mostly to talk to girls. I remember I had a friend who used to read my text messages to me, and when he was reading, I would ask him, what is this word? What is that one? He would tell me and I'd bank them in my memory. Then I'd save those messages, and use them as a prompt for later on. So when someone sent me a message saying *What's up? Where are you?* I'd remember the message that I had saved that my friend read to me earlier. I could respond with that.

Mind you, I'd still usually give one- or two-word answers. *Sup? Cool. K.* It was an easy way to communicate. But I was driven because I was trying to message girls. I was a kid, that was a priority. I wasn't going to put myself completely out there, but I wanted to communicate enough to meet people.

Now, as I got older and I began teaching myself, I wanted to go beyond that. My partner bought me a book of quotes (see chapter 5), and she would read to me. I had basic reading skills, maybe a first- or second-grade level at that time, so I could read simple words and stuff, but it was hard to understand and break down the pieces of a sentence or paragraph and comprehend. She would read to me slowly so I could follow along and it made it easier.

I also listened to a crap ton of audio books, and that helped me start understanding sentence structures. After listening, I'd read some of the books, at my own pace. It took me about two years to finish that quote book (it is *long*). I would go through each quote and put a star next to words or circle them so I could remember what I was reading. Then I could refer back to them and put together the words and meanings.

These were some of my main methods for learning to read. But I would say the *best* tool for progress, for me, was voice to text, because I was able to talk to the phone and see the words pop up in real time. This skyrocketed my reading level, which jumped enormously. And since I could do voice to text on my own time in private, I really began to learn instead of just memorizing. If I said *I love you, I can't wait to see you later on*, I could see those words, understand them, and be able to reuse them even without cutting and pasting. That made it really easy for me to recognize and really comprehend what I was saying at the same time.

Today I have a reading specialist who helps me, who I will be studying with for two hours a day for about four months. She says she can tell that I learned from memorizing because I don't completely know many words—so I need to combine memorization and comprehension. It's a little complicated to explain because it's all new to me but that's the gist of it. I'm learning to be able to use words as tools, instead of only recognizing them as symbols.

At first I wasn't reading adult novels or anything like that. It was kid's books, young adult books, school books. Sometimes I would read songs. I would pull up songs on Spotify and I would sing the lyrics, but read them at the same time, singing them on TikTok Live. A one-man karaoke. That ended up giving me a lot of motivation because people out there cheered me on. It was like a sport—it's always easier to play the sport when you've got fans in the bleachers. When there are people in a full stadium rooting for you, it makes you want to play your hardest. So to me, when I was in there reading, it could be uncomfortable sometimes because I was struggling in front of everyone. But I kept going, because they carried me.

Eventually I got used to the feeling of people knowing that I couldn't read. I was no longer uncomfortable. In fact, it even became fun. I'd go live to read and a couple hundred people were in there. Luckily a lot of them were educators, and they would help me a lot and walk me through it. It was like having a one-on-one tutor, but instead of having one, I got a hundred one-on-one tutors. That made it *so* much more fun.

Some people would even download books I was reading and read with me. If I got a word wrong, they'd break it down for me, and spell it out in a way I could understand. If there were silent letters, which are much harder to learn later in life than you'd think, they would explain the rules so I could understand and take it forward. Not everyone has an audience ready to cheer them on; I was really fortunate. That's why it pays to share even if it's embarrassing.

I'm not pretending I've learned everything there is to know about the rules of grammar and all; I'm still building my confidence in that. There are a lot of ways for a person to go about learning to read, regardless of their age, and I probably went about it one of the harder ways. But it all boils down to learning and practicing until it becomes natural. This is where I am now, but by the time we're all at the end of this book, I'll be better.

That's how it works.

1

READING IS A BEGINNING

The Giver (1993), by Lois Lowry

I HADN'T EVEN POSTED THE VIDEO YET, but I had so rarely said those words in my life, and already it felt like something started to lift off my shoulders.

I might as well have been saying I didn't know how to use a spoon. Everything else about me seems pretty normal—I can walk around and have conversations, make my meals, go to work but yeah, there's this essential thing I can't do. Even little kids take basic reading and writing skills for granted—they can scribble *I Love You* on a handmade card to their mom in first grade. I was going to have to work my way *up* to that. That's how far behind I was. Because without reading, there's no writing.

Believe me, being unable to read is a *major* disadvantage in this world. Maybe that sounds obvious, or maybe it sounds like something you can easily step around. But nah. If you've ever tried to read a sign in another country where not only the language is different, but the alphabet is, too, you have a tiny idea of what being illiterate is like. It affects every part of daily life.

Of course, it wasn't like I suddenly heard about illiteracy at thirty-two. All my life I'd known I had that limitation. How did I get here, to this age, unable to read to begin with? How had I hidden it so well, for so long? Who didn't notice? Who did?

There is no easy answer. People often assume it was the school system that failed me. And it did, but it's not that simple. It's easy to look at a Black kid raised by a single mom in Pennsylvania and guess what happened to keep him ignorant. And while my education, or lack thereof, was a big part of it, it's so much more than that. So many things had to go wrong for me to make it that far without this crucial skill, and then so many things had to go right and wrong and right for me to *want* it. To crave it. To demand it of myself.

Truth is, I was a seed planted in bad soil. It's hard to grow without proper nourishment: figuratively *and* literally. My sister and I had gone hungry more times than not growing up. I wasn't getting enough academic help in school. I also struggled with OCD and ADHD, and the school system provided no emotional or mental health support for a kid in trouble. I was told that it was just me "acting out." Eventually, I would also suffer from PTSD as well.

My surroundings were too chaotic and unstable for me to think or care about reading. School wasn't the safe space it should've been, and it left me in survival mode.

A lack of education can have repercussions that the uneducated often don't have the resources to understand. I managed to go to community college. And just as quickly, everything fell apart when crimes I committed—through ignorance, not malice—caught up with me.

We'll come back to the story of prison in a little bit.

Like I said, I knew some words from texting; I recognized them, but I couldn't *read.* When I opened a book, I could see the words, even some I knew. But it was incomprehensible when the words were strung together. It's like singing along to a popular song in a foreign language, like "La Bamba" for a non-Spanish speaker. You can sing most of the words, and maybe you know what a few of them mean, but overall, you have no idea what the song is saying. That's where I was with reading in 2020. I'd be reading without understanding what I was reading. Story eluded me. Tone, nuance, and subtext were beyond me. Therefore, I think, I couldn't even grasp the story of my own life. The how, the why, the future.

Learning to read literally sent me to the hospital, as you'll learn later. But my experiences have taught me how important it is to make changes—even when they're terrifying or difficult. I wanted more for myself, for my partner, and for my son. So I decided to do something about it. And the world that's since opened up before me is unbelievably bright.

Never in a million years did I think I'd end up where I'm at today: a TikTok influencer and literacy advocate based out of California with an actual book out with my name on the cover.

People ask me all the time, "How'd you get here?"

And I respond, "Man, I just started reading."

I hope people use my story, the mistakes I've made, and the lessons I've learned along the way as a guide. I hope this book will help you achieve your own goals. Whether you love to read or hate it, whether you're just learning how to read or have been reading forever, I hope this book helps you to become the best version of yourself.

And I hope it encourages you to do scary things.

I did it. I'm still doing it! And learning to read on TikTok was the catalyst. (I like that word; I like using more words.)

Throughout *this* book, I'll recommend *the other books* I've read that changed my life, and that reflect the lessons I've learned—kicking off with *The Giver* by Lois Lowry.

* * *

In *The Giver*, the citizens have no knowledge of the past, or of choice. The Giver of the title—a wise older man who holds the world's memories—introduces the main character, Jonas, to freedom and knowledge. By introducing myself to reading, I also gained knowledge of an unknown world, and realized that it belongs to me too.

The Giver, also known as the "Receiver of Memory," initially shares happy memories—everyday sweet moments—with Jonas, which Jonas relishes. This echoed the beginning of my reading journey, where I started simply and was basically a blank slate. Then the old man transmits painful memories—such as of hunger and war—that traumatize Jonas. Reading this reminded me of my own anxiety. How it was comfortable, in a way, to know less. Growing was *uncomfortable.* I felt a deep connection between my own experiences and a fictional character for the first time. *The Giver* perfectly captured the overwhelm of not knowing something and then having it being pushed dramatically into your life—as if by magic.

The book dives into Jonas's suffering, into the *why* of it all; in a way it mirrored why I suffered so much as I began to understand. Jonas keeps going; he needs the knowledge. *The Giver* demonstrates why it *does* ultimately feel better to know. Knowledge is a part of Jonas's life now. He can't look back and pretend he doesn't know what he knows. Every time I look back on my ignorance in a nostalgic way, I remind myself that I can't go back even if I want to.

Thinking about this book now, I think it was actually the Giver, not Jonas, who impacted me most. Jonas underwent a similar transformation to mine, but I already knew my side of the story. The Giver—who represented the history of humankind—was jaded but goodhearted; he shared his perspective while caring for someone in my position, a position of receiving. This felt reassuring. It was something I could trust. The story made me feel like there was someone who believed in the person I am and the path I was on.

Reading introduced me to freedom, and I know it will allow me to have the independence I've always longed for. Think about what you need to free yourself and remember that you always have a choice.

I'm excited that you're here with me. I've had so many kind people help me along the way, and I've been changed by the stories I've read. I hope my story changes your life for the better too.

If there's one thing reading has taught me, it's that there is a story in everything, and if you want to understand a character, you're going to have to get an idea of where they come from.

So let's start at the beginning.

2

READING IS A KINGDOM

The Phantom Tollbooth (1961), by Norton Juster,
with illustrations by Jules Feiffer

I GREW UP IN BETHLEHEM, PENNSYLVANIA, with my mom and older sister, in a neighborhood called Livingston. While Bethlehem was a historic town with a lot of landmarks and flavor from colonial and Revolutionary War times, it wasn't a well-kept tourist destination. It was no Philly. Today it's being rebuilt with nicer housing, restaurants, shops, and so on, but back in the 1990s it was barely hanging on.

Livingston was its poorest corner—kind of like a project outside of the projects. A sub-project. There were some single houses, but most of us lived in old brick row houses. It was also a Puerto Rican neighborhood, so as a Black family, we were on a bit of an island there too. But living there introduced me to a lot I wouldn't have otherwise known. Puerto Rican music, food, and traditions. Puerto Ricans, especially the ones who immigrated, have a culture all their own that I love.

The way I remember it, life was great. In my memories, it was always bright and sunny; I was always outside. The block was full of kids, and we were always playing. When you think of the projects it sounds depressing, full of bullies and crime and conflict. But it was like any other area filled with kids. I had a real childhood with some wonderful moments. Hot summers, snow days, playing ball.

I grew up with my mom and sister. I mean it when I say we grew together. We were all figuring it out the best we could, and my mom's priority was making sure that we all survived. Food on the table. Roof over our heads. She depended a lot on the school to keep us safe and out of trouble. She trusted the school system completely for our education.

My mother always stressed the importance of school. She always told us we had to go, but I never understood that it was *so you can learn how to keep up in this world.* To me it always seemed like she was saying, *Go to school or else you'll go to jail.* School seemed like something *they* made us do. Whoever *they* were. There was an intensity behind her instruction, a looming threat of *or else*. Everyone knows *or else* must be unimaginably bad. That kind of pressure made an impact on me from the beginning. School and fear were linked.

TV and movies always show inspiring, scrappy teachers and kindhearted administrators fighting for us. That's what I wished for more than anything. One single adult who understood the system, saw me, and knew how to help move me through it. Someone fighting for me. To help me be better, get smarter, and make it out more than just alive. To thrive even.

Nope.

The teachers and administrators at my school had no idea what to do with me. It would be easy to say they didn't know my home life or my background, and to them I was merely a pain-in-the-ass kid they had to put up with until they could finally push me on to the next grade. That's how it felt.

In truth, I was always up to some antic or another—walking around the halls when I should have been in class, talking back and arguing instead of being more respectful of my elders. I was learning, all right.

I was learning what I could get away with. Learning how to do my own thing. How to push boundaries. Learning who cared.

Instead of figuring out why I was behaving this way and reacting accordingly, my elementary school's solutions were like this: They'd put my desk in the principal's office. Yeah. For a while, every day, I'd head to my desk in the office with a bag lunch and my work. That's how school started for me. Isolated, without a teacher.

I was treated like a problem, so I *became* a problem. Or *more* of a problem. Since nobody could teach me, I never learned the basics of getting along in a society, much less the importance of reading and writing. I got left behind. I had ADHD, though I hadn't yet been diagnosed with it, so I couldn't sit still. And trust me, all the principal wants you to do is sit still if you're made to be in his office.

From everything I know now, it seems like school usually works like this: you go in, you learn some things, you're given homework to do at home, your teacher tells you what you missed and fills in any gaps, eventually you take a quiz, then a test, then you move on to the next thing. You learn something, you secure it in your brain, then you get the next piece. Something like that, anyway. I'm only guessing from what I've figured out since, because that is not how my school worked. We were given a packet, and in that packet would be your whole years' worth of assignments. You'd keep going through the pages as the days went on. Our teachers never *taught*. You were kind of expected to know things, and the teacher could assist, but not if you had no foundation. It felt like we came in every day and sat for a test, with teachers there only to clarify. If that.

If I asked questions, if anyone asked questions, it felt like we were dragging everyone else down. Like, *why doesn't this kid know?*

Most kids don't want to stand out, and I didn't either. I didn't like to put a spotlight on myself. If I missed something, I missed it. Only eventually I had missed so much foundation that all my walls were falling down.

Look, I'm not stupid. Not now, and not then, either. I was uneducated. Which, you know, we all are as kids. We're in school to be educated. I *wanted* to be taught. I expected to be. But I wasn't.

School days were endless, let me tell you. Six hours of paralyzing boredom. I sat there under the buzzing fluorescent lights, not knowing how to do anything, twiddling my thumbs, counting the ceiling panels, knocking on my desk, struggling to sit still because I couldn't learn anything in that environment. And I didn't have enough familiarity with the class subjects to even make guesses. It was painful.

To this day, the smell of pencil shavings and paper makes me anxious.

The first time I remember realizing the difference between me and the other kids was after getting suspended for the first time. I had missed days, and then when I returned to the classroom, I didn't know what everyone else already knew; I had missed a lot and gotten too far behind to catch up. At the start of class, everybody pulled out their books and began reading. Not only that, they understood the stories. They could answer the teacher's questions about the words. I couldn't.

If I hadn't lost my academic way, it probably wouldn't have been nearly as bad. I can remember the feeling of *getting it* when I learned to do a math problem. Understanding what you're doing makes it not only easier but almost fun. Like a puzzle. Puzzles are fun when you know how to do them.

But imagine trying to do the Sunday *New York Times* crossword puzzle in Greek or Polish. As if it isn't already difficult, but now, with an impossible obstacle.

Every day that I remained behind in learning, learning got that much harder for me until finally I was helplessly and hopelessly lost. It was the worst feeling. I would look around and even the kids I always thought of as lazy, kids who only sat around and threw spitballs at the ceiling, somehow were managing to answer questions and get their tests and homework back with green writing instead of red. Suddenly (and it did feel sudden) it seemed like I had been dropped in the middle of a country where I couldn't understand the language or make any sense of the alphabet. The expression *it's all Greek to me* applied because I didn't understand anything going on around me.

So, I shut down.

That was it for me. From that moment on, I used the *shutdown* method every single day. After a while, the school began to have regular meetings with my mom about my behavior. When nothing changed, the administrators expelled me and sent me to another school for special education. I was in second grade. That's just a little kid, you know? That was a chance to catch me before I fell too far through the cracks but instead, they let go.

And so, yeah, I believed I was special—in a bad way. It sounded to me like they were saying I was stupid and bad, and I believed it. Not because I was in special education, but because the teasing from other kids and the attitude of the chaperones reinforced it. Overall, I think we're getting nicer as a society, but back then kids were ruthless. Anything that made you different made you weird. The bus jokes were endless; the "SPED" teasing was cruel; and there was a lot of pointing, laughing, and mocking.

I started to think the students outside of special ed already *did* know everything. There was a *me* and a *them*. Then the special ed kids, *us*, and the "regular kids," *them*. Even though it seems so obvious now, the way it appeared to me then was that everyone else was just born *that* way and I was born *this* way. Like how some kids might have a big house and a whole family complete with two parents, and I had what I had (which was . . . not that, and I'll get into it later). I thought they went to school because it was the normal thing to do, not because it had any value. I thought they were born with secret information that made all of it make sense, and I was born without it. As if they were sharpening, polishing, honing who they were, and I was so behind that I didn't even have the *who I am* part.

In special ed, I was surrounded by kids with a bunch of different needs. There were kids with developmental issues, kids in wheelchairs. Some had loud tantrums, some needed physical assistance.

Sometimes it felt like we were being hidden away so we wouldn't distract everyone else. If normal school had felt like teaching and learning wasn't the point, then this was ten times worse. The teachers were stressed, always managing some outburst or problem. They were nice, those adults, but it felt like there wasn't enough time in the day to take care of everyone and *also* learn things like counting, what math is; and letters, words, and what they mean.

I acted out a lot. It wasn't big stuff, just a bored kid in a room with a lot of chaos and teachers talking about things he didn't understand. You know how it is. Children want attention, and they'll get it somehow.

So what I got was kicked out of school in fifth grade, then again in sixth or seventh, and then I was sent to another school around eighth or ninth grade and stayed there. I wish I could be more specific, but the whole thing was more a series of punishments and conversations in small rooms with paper-stacked desks, so I can't say for sure. I think other kids were out there looking forward to different milestones, and I was simply trying to stay afloat. How are you going to care about pep rallies and who to take to junior prom when you're barely keeping your head above water? Well, you don't.

And yeah, it didn't help that I was Black. Or that I was poor. It didn't help that I lived in the projects, where even there I was kind of a cultural outsider. I looked like the characters my teachers saw on TV, the ones that were supposed to be bad. Rappers. Criminals. They often treated me like I was a thug. Was I? No! I was a kid. My rebellion was because everything was so *hard*. Harder than it should have been. I never could sit still, pay attention, and I was so behind, and I felt jealous of all the other kids. Why were they all so much better at everything? How come it was so easy for them? I thought it just so happened that none of the other students ever had a bad day. I resented everyone around me who had more than I did too, so I wasn't exactly a joy to have in class.

Either way, wherever I was, I was pretty much in special ed the entire time up until I graduated. There were some good people who tried to help. People who were nice to me. It was all a mess, and they were only trying their best.

Despite everything, I always *passed*. Always.

Isn't that crazy?

I never failed a grade. If I was learning something, it was how to get by, get through, get past obstacles. I wasn't learning math, science, or reading. But I was learning how to keep going. How to slip through the cracks.

Before connecting with people online who've had similar experiences (which would take me more than a decade to do), I didn't have anyone I could share this experience with. I don't actually know if any of the kids I grew up with couldn't read. If so, they'd have been hiding it the same way that I was. It was something none of us had much interest in—none of us cared about reading that much, so it didn't come up. Any of my friends who could read probably did it for school only. It wasn't in the culture to sit around talking about reading. That felt like school stuff, and for the most part, our mantra was *kids hate school* and anything that feels like it. I was years away from seeing reading as a luxury or a hobby. Unthinkable to me back then.

So, yeah, if my peers couldn't read, they hid it. Sometimes I'd stumble into a conversation about it with someone—them saying something like, *yeah it sucks when everyone thinks you're dumb* and I'd agree—but we wouldn't get into any of the darker parts. Nothing about the way we were treated, or what illiteracy was doing to us on a deeper level. I think it's like some untreated people who have anxiety or depression talking to one another. You don't go too deep into the specifics of your experience, but you still have that mutual understanding and make small talk around it without the tools to address it. Again, we're growing as a society and people talk more about their feelings but in the hood? In the '90s and 2000s? Ha, no.

Hiding definitely became a part of my life. My goal wasn't to thrive, it was to get through with the least amount of friction possible. To survive.

By the time I got to my senior year in high school, texting was popular and that was an issue for me. It was a huge problem. Texting obviously means reading *and* writing, so I was screwed. This reading thing was affecting my social life. It was an important form of communication, especially with girls. You're telling me that *reading* was why I couldn't get a girlfriend?

I had to have friends read and write my texts for me, and they couldn't always be around to do that. What I ended up doing was mixing and matching messages my friends read out to me with other messages I got. It was a lot of memorization. Again, learning, but not the right way.

They weren't long messages; at that age it was usually something like, "Hey, what's up?" I'd show that message to a friend and they would explain that the message said, "What's up?" I could remember that. From there, when I went to read another message, whether it was long or short, I could see the "Hey, what's up?" in there, and understand at least that. So, a girl could've texted me, "Hey, I just got home from school, gonna get something to eat. What's up?" and I would have read in that whole message, "Hey, . . . what's up?" And I'd probably have just sent "What's up?" right back.

Texting literally taught me the rudiments of how to read. Patterns, letter shapes, repetition. Other than that, I'd never learned. So from that moment, all the way until I was thirty-two years old, I learned how to read through text messages.

Unfortunately, this didn't build strong communication skills, and I still struggle with being misunderstood and misunderstanding others today. There are a lot of things I get in trouble with relationship-wise because I'll read or send something the wrong way. Tone is something I haven't locked down. My partner will read something back to me in the middle of an argument, from a conversation we had, and I'll realize she read something *into* what I said that wasn't what I meant. Or I'll have sent something I didn't mean. Then I need to backpedal and be like, "Okay, I didn't mean that. That was the total opposite of what I was saying." But it's frustrating because I know what I meant. To me, I said what I meant. Still, it's not easy to take it back.

There are many conversations I've had like that and still do to this day. For my whole entire life, I've had conversations that other people don't understand, and I've felt so alone because of it. It's exactly like it was in school, where life was one way for others and a totally different, hard way for me. I had so little control.

For instance: how I came across to people.

When you're trying to make it through a conversation in a language you barely understand, there's always the possibility of saying the absolute wrong thing and not even knowing it. I mean, how many times in movies has the silly American said something comically inappropriate to someone in a foreign country? I wasn't exactly mixing up the bathroom and the library, but I was answering with one-word replies (which made me seem like I didn't care), I wasn't answering at all (because I was overwhelmed, but it probably seemed like I wasn't interested), or I misunderstood (which made it seem like I didn't care enough to pay attention).

It created shame in me and led me to be dependent on others, to lack independence. Not being able to read meant I couldn't have the life other people had, even in basic terms. I was isolated. By others, by my inability, and by myself. All of this led me to be a person I wasn't all that proud of.

I felt like a stranger, a foreigner, a traveler from another land in my own life.

I didn't read *The Phantom Tollbooth* when I was a kid. I wish I had, so that I would have connected with the main character, Milo—an unbelievably bored kid, so bored he can't stand it. Then he's transported to a land where there are all these made-up names and words—I get that! When you can't read, all words kind of feel made up. I'm pretty much taking your word for it that the word *knock* has a bunch of *k*s in it, that when I look at a jumble of letters like *bouquet*, it means a handful of flowers. This book was a challenge for me when I did eventually read it, because I was playing catch-up on real words. But I powered through, stayed committed, and my strength as a reader grew because of it.

This boy, Milo, was on an adventure to save the kingdom of knowledge. By educating himself, he is able to defeat the *demons of ignorance*. Learning to read, as I would eventually one day do, I had to face down a lot of demons.

Where we are in my story, just a lost kid in Bethlehem, I was a long time away from my own adventure to find knowledge. But if I could do it over, if I could parent myself, I would have had myself read *The Phantom Tollbooth* when I was in school. Middle school maybe. And while it may have been written for kids, I guarantee that anyone who reads this book can relate to it.

You're never too old, too far behind, or too uneducated to travel to the kingdom of knowledge.

3

READING IS FREEDOM

Holes (1998), by Louis Sachar

For me, it all came to a head when I was nineteen years old. There's no cute way to lead into this so I'll just say it: I was trafficking guns, and I honestly had no idea that I could go to jail for it.

For a while there, my life consisted of buying guns and selling them for a profit. I was a middleman, not the brains behind the operation, but I did it, nonetheless.

See, I thought it was only a crime to traffic drugs. *Everyone* knows that about drugs, right? There are TV shows about people sewing illegal substances into the false bottom of a suitcase or strapping drugs to their bodies. There've been a million movies about drug traffickers getting stopped by the good guys. Obviously, drug trafficking is a big concern for law enforcement. But guns were so commonplace around me that I didn't even think about it. Yeah, I know, this sounds crazy, but a lack of education has a huge effect on every aspect of your life. The newspapers and headlines scrolling by on TV might have said a lot about gun laws, but I didn't know anything about those laws.

As I was not able to read, I was mostly focused on what was happening *right here, right now*. I got my cues from the people around me, so if I got lied to or someone didn't have the accurate information, I wouldn't know. Not being able to read prevented me from getting an education, even on the streets. I was learning from anyone who was motivated to teach me, and there was no guarantee that those "teachers" were always good guys. Not if they had an incentive for me to believe something.

Ignorance is not an excuse, I know that, but it is strange, isn't it? What we're taught is what we learn. What we learn is what we know. I knew what I was doing was okay. Normal.

Obviously, I was dead wrong.

After high school, everyone went off to college or work or whatever they were going to do. Even though I hated school, I was worried about getting even more left behind. There was no way I would be able to get into a real college or university, where standards were high and only a certain percentage of kids could make it in. My big lie would have been blown out of the water on the first day.

Instead, I enrolled in a local community college, which wasn't as demanding or competitive. I wanted to know more things; I thought college might be different.

To apply, I went to an administrative building at the school. I didn't have to tell the woman there anything; she could tell that I needed her help without me telling her. I remember her handing me a sheet of paper and me just looking at her blankly, going, "I don't know what to do." And she helped me, guiding me through the whole application. Told me where to put my name, where to put my address, everything. I plugged in the shapes and symbols I had memorized, which I knew represented that information.

The way people spoke about college and student loans sounded like a perfect solution to my problems. Student loans were supposedly easy to get, and low interest. That's how people talked about them back then, or at least that's what I was told. Again, I couldn't exactly do the research myself. Having a degree at the end of it was supposed to mean I'd get thousands more for the same job I'd be doing anyway. It felt like it was a train I could hop on to get from point A to point B. I hoped maybe things would get brighter after point B.

My friends and my sister told me that when you're broke and living in the hood, you can get grants. Grants means money. And you can use that money to buy the stuff you need. I thought this could help me. Maybe I could live in cheap student housing; maybe school would give me some structure. I'd seen movies. I had an idea of what that could look like.

In class, when I was on my own without someone I trusted to lead me through, I just followed everyone else. It's amazing how far nodding along and joining in on a laugh can get you.

It was tough, though, I'm not gonna lie to you. Not being able to keep up and faking it is exhausting. But it was only a couple of years. I could get through it. Then I would have something to make my life better. I'd been getting by my whole life; I had a high school diploma to prove it. What if I could get a college degree? That would say something about me. While it might mean to some people that I was smart and educated, what it would really mean was, *I will always find a way to do what I gotta do.*

That's a good guy to hire, right?

It was a perfect plan! But, yeah, it didn't work out like that.

So I was in school, trying to be good. Then I was at the barbershop one day at this place I'd been going to for haircuts for years, and this guy approached me. He was a cool dude—at least, that's how he seemed to me. After one of my cuts, he asked me if I wanted to run an errand for him. He offered me some cash for it, and being young and desperate, I figured, *why not?* People did stuff like that where I'm from. Quick bucks here and there. A lot of cash going around.

So I drove him someplace about five minutes away and he gave me two hundred bucks. He basically said there was more where that came from, if I was looking to make more money. Like I said, I was young, dumb, and looking for purpose, so I was like, *hell* yeah. Two hundred bucks for a few miles' drive? Why wouldn't I say yes to more fast money?

He said, "Can you pick up a package and drop it off somewhere?" I didn't even ask what was in the package. I knew better; kids like me knew better than to poke around the details.

So, I did it. It was easy money. He kept asking me to do small jobs like that, paying me a couple hundred bucks here and there. I was merely doing him favors, and it was kinda like, "Okay, cool." I'd pick up packages or give him rides to places, and I kept getting paid for it. I didn't think much of it; I figured it was some side hustle, nothing major. Maybe some weed or whatever. And this went on for a few weeks, maybe a month, at most. He told me eventually what was in the bags—guns. Once I knew what was going on, I still didn't go to the cops. I just kept doing what I was told.

But what I didn't know was that the guy wasn't merely a dude in the neighborhood. Turns out, he was an undercover fed. And none of the stuff he had me involved in was actually going to the streets. He was using me as part of a sting operation. I was being watched the whole time. But at the time, I had no idea. I was only a kid trying to make a little gas money and help out my mom.

Being raised like I was—by a struggling single mother—wasn't uncommon in my neighborhood. It wasn't a rich area, that's for sure, and there were a lot of rough situations we had to deal with. From day one, I was exposed to crime, drugs, and violence. That was the reality where I grew up. It wasn't shocking; it was normal.

I was used to seeing people dealing drugs, fighting, and making poor choices. And, I can't lie, I did a whole lot of those things myself. But there was always this part of me that knew it wasn't right. I knew if I got caught doing certain things, I could end up in a whole lot of trouble.

That didn't stop everyone around me, though. Friends, older brothers, and even parents were deep into that life. It wasn't always a choice; sometimes, it felt like you had no alternative but to be involved. It was what it was.

I didn't set out to be a drug dealer. I really didn't want that life for myself, not deep down. Like I said, I thought of myself as more of a middleman, but now I realize I was just in denial. I think that's how it goes for a lot of people who get swept up in that world.

Then one day—a whole year after that day at the barbershop—I was hanging out at my mom's house, doing nothing special. It was a quiet afternoon. Suddenly, the feds kicked the door down. I mean, they literally smashed it open, no polite knock first to ask if they had the right house. It was like something out of a movie—there must have been ten guys coming in the front door and ten guys coming in the back door, all with guns drawn and pointed. In seconds, the house erupted into a storm of leather boots on wood, whooshing windbreakers, and shouting. They marched in, pulled me out of my bed, knocked me and my mom down to the ground, and arrested us both.

They didn't even tell me what was going on at first. They started asking, "Where are the guns? Where are the drugs?"

The whole thing was a lot bigger than me. No one was after me; there were major criminals they wanted to nail. I just happened to get caught in the crossfire.

I was arrested for the "intent" of committing a crime. I felt framed; I wouldn't have been anywhere near that situation if it wasn't for the man in the barbershop.

It was a weird situation. I hadn't done anything wrong until an undercover federal agent asked me to. It's like I had been tested in a way, but I had failed.

I spent a month in jail before I was released on bail. I had barely enough time to finish up my year of community college—somehow, the system moves that slow. But then when sentencing finally came, about a year after that, they hit me with fifty-four months in prison. Memorial Day weekend 2011 is when I got that sentence.

That was when one of the biggest benefits of school became clear to me. It bought me time because the court let me finish my year in school before I began my sentence. I'm so grateful they did, because that one year ultimately led me to my purpose; it planted a dream in my mind. I took a speech communication class where I gave a speech about going to prison, and how I felt about it. The feeling I got speaking in front of that class got me thinking: *I could be more than who I currently was.* For the first time, I was using words and people were listening. They wanted to hear me. I could express myself and make a difference.

It was there that I realized that I wanted to become a motivational speaker, a passion I still have today. But I knew I had a long way to go. You can't speak if you have nothing to say.

I'm grateful I got to finish out that year, but while everyone around me was getting ready to drive to the beach and party, I was handing over my clothes and freedom and putting on a jumpsuit.

I had more than four years of prison ahead of me. It was too much to even think about.

I was sent to the Federal Detention Center in Philadelphia. That's where I had to report, get processed, and wait. Then, after that, I got moved around to different places—kept in different facilities for weeks at a time while I was being transferred. Eventually, I ended up in a federal prison in Atlanta, and then I was sent to Manchester, Kentucky, where I spent eighteen months.

Most of that transferring time, though, was spent in solitary confinement.

The hole.

Alone, with nothing but my own racing thoughts. My own regret, anger, frustration; my OCD and ADHD—both of which I'd been diagnosed with by this time but had been given no tools to manage. They were just two more things that were wrong with me.

So after a lifetime of not being able to sit still, now I had no choice. I'd be trapped, with nothing to do, for years.

Why? Because when you're transferring between prisons, they don't always have an open cell waiting on the other end for you right away. You end up sitting alone in a holding cell, waiting. And it's not like I was the only one. A lot of prisoners go through this. You just wait—alone.

It was brutal. I felt like I was losing my mind, and I think I was. I've been recently diagnosed with PTSD, and I think for sure it must stem from this period. Some days, I'd lie there, too overwhelmed to do anything. Other days, I'd try to stay busy. I'd do push-ups, to pass the time. And I'd try to sleep whenever I could. I would panic sometimes, but somehow, I never cried or lost my composure. I'm here to tell you, a lot of people there did. Prison isn't designed to be pleasant. At least not the prisons that we regular folk get sent to; I don't know about people like Martha Stewart.

The experience froze me. I think it was that I couldn't even find the space to break down. I'm still figuring out how to handle it. It was a tough ordeal.

After eighteen months in federal prison in Kentucky, I requested a transfer, if only for a change of scenery, and I ended up in a prison in New Jersey to finish out my sentence. But even that wasn't easy. Not at all. I had to go through the whole transfer process again. That meant two more months in solitary as I moved from one place to the next. Again.

I was the youngest person in the prison when I got to Kentucky. I was about twenty, maybe twenty-one years old at the time. Honestly, when I first walked in, I thought I had a good handle on things. I thought I knew a lot, you know? I'd been through some stuff, had lived through a lot of crazy situations. But the truth was, I was pretty ignorant about what prison life would be like. No one really can understand it until you're actually there.

I had to learn fast. The first thing I did when I got there was just watch. I paid close attention to everything around me, trying to figure out the rules that didn't get told to you. I kept quiet. You don't want to come in and start running your mouth when you're new, especially being a young guy. You don't know who's looking at you, who's sizing you up, or what kind of reputation you're about to make for yourself. I kept to myself a lot. I didn't talk much; I tried to lie low and figure things out.

I also made sure to keep myself in good shape. I had been working out a lot before I got locked up, and I wasn't a small guy by any means. But prison? It'll make you want to stay in shape even more. The way you look, the way you carry yourself, it matters. And all you've got is time.

I worked out constantly—push-ups, pull-ups, squats, whatever I could do with the little equipment they had. It wasn't only about staying strong physically; it was also about keeping my mind sharp. When you're locked up, you need to find ways to stay sane. The routine of exercising gave me something to focus on. It kept me grounded.

But prison wasn't all about physical strength. There was a lot more to it, a lot of stuff you'd never think about if you've never been inside. One of the worst things I remember from my time there was when I had to get a root canal. Yeah, you heard that right—a root canal in prison. And it wasn't only once. It happened twice.

Man, it was awful. I still feel ill just thinking about it. The pain was intense—no kidding, it felt like someone was drilling into my skull. And the worst part? They didn't give me any medicine to numb the ache before the root canal. No ibuprofen, no painkillers, nothing. I was sitting there, sweating and aching, trying not to scream. I remember feeling like I was losing my mind from the pain. Even when I finally got the root canal—because they don't always have the best equipment or the best people working on you—it was torture. There, I ended up crying, not because I wanted to, but because I had no choice—it was my body crying, not me. It was that bad.

That whole experience was a big wake-up call about how dependent you become when you're in prison. You're stuck relying on everyone else, whether you want to or not. That experience wasn't totally new to me, obviously, but in there it was so much worse. You can't just run to the corner store and grab some Advil when you're hurting. You can't simply buy whatever you need, like you would in the real world. You don't get those little comforts anymore. If you need something, you're at the mercy of the system, and that's a humbling thing to realize. It's only you, your cell, and whatever the system decides to give you.

That lack of control over your own health is a whole different level of helplessness. You can't even go to a doctor the way you want to. If you're sick, you have to wait for someone else to decide if you deserve treatment or not. You're completely dependent on the staff there. If you're lucky and you play the game right (and no one will tell you the rules), they'll take care of you. But if you're not, you're left to suffer. And trust me, I wasn't the only one going through it. A lot of the guys in there had health problems, and not all of them got the care they needed. You see a lot of people struggling with things that could've been easily treated on the outside, but in prison? You're left to sit with it. And that feeling, that dependency—it's one of those things you can't forget. It eats at you. It's not just about the physical stuff, either. It messes with your head. You start feeling like you don't have a say in anything.

I had been through something similar, being in the special ed classes. The people in charge have so many demands that almost no one gets what they actually need.

Man, I thought school was bad. Little did I know I'd end up here, in prison, where everything was so much worse.

So yeah, having dental problems so bad that I needed a root canal and not getting any pain relief was brutal. But it was more than just the pain. It was the realization of how much you're at the mercy of the system. It made me think about everything I took for granted before.

The lack of control over your own life—it sticks with you. You go through it, you deal with it, and you move on. But you don't forget it. It's one of those lessons that you carry with you, and you keep it in the back of your mind every time you face a situation where you have some control over your life. You learn to appreciate the little things.

Obviously, a lot of prison is tough. A lot of it is straight-up miserable. It's not a place you want to be, and it's definitely not a place where anything is handed to you. But you know what? I want to speak on the good parts too. The truth is, there are some real good people in prison. It's easy to forget that when you're caught up in the worst parts of it, but if you look closely enough, you'll see that there's a lot of humanity still there. There are always good people, even in places like that. You just have to be open to it.

I met some great guys out there in Kentucky. No matter what they did to get there. Prison has a way of making people who want a better life decide not to keep doing the shit that put them in prison. And there are different levels of how "bad" everyone was. But we all had one thing in common: We fucked up. One way or another. Even the innocent folks—and of course most people said they were innocent. They still had a time they could look to where it all went wrong. Where they could have done something different.

The first week I was in there, I didn't know what to expect. It was all new to me. I was trying to figure it out, keep my head down, and not make waves. But then this guy comes up to me one day. He looks at me, sizing me up for a second, and then says, "Hey, I need to tell you something."

I can't lie, that was a pretty scary moment. He could have been ready to tell me he was going to strangle me with his bare hands. There wasn't much I could do to get away no matter what. He might have been another dude looking for someone to do his dirty work. And I knew how good that had turned out.

"I'm gonna give you some lessons," he said.

"What do you mean?" This still didn't sound promising.

He gave a little shrug. "You look like somebody who doesn't want to get into too much trouble, so I'm gonna help you out."

I was standing there, still kind of confused but also grateful that someone was willing to talk to me. And then he hit me with the first lesson:

"Don't trust nobody in here," he told me, straight up. "I'm being serious. Don't trust nobody. You gotta be careful who you talk to, who you let in. People will say anything to get close to you. They'll use you. And trust me, you don't want to get caught up in that."

He was talking like he knew exactly what he was saying. He wasn't some old-timer, but there was a certain weight to his words. It was like he'd seen enough to know that I needed to hear it. And I believed him.

"Don't tell anybody about your case, your life, nothing. Don't give them any information. Even the smallest thing, someone will figure out a way to flip it on you. They'll use whatever they can to make your time worse or get themselves out of trouble. You could get in a whole lot of trouble talking too much, building up a case for someone else, or giving them ammo to take you down."

He wasn't wrong. That's the game in prison. People are always trying to get over on you, always looking for an angle. It's not only about the guards. It's about the guys around you too. They're all trying to look out for themselves, and if you're not careful, you can end up helping someone else get ahead while you get stuck. Not a place with a whole lot of trust.

"If you start talking too much, people will turn on you. They'll tell on you, maybe try to get some less time for themselves, or they'll twist something you said. You think you're just talking, but it's not like that in here."

I was feeling kind of good that someone cared enough to help me out like this. Then he added, "Even when I walk away, don't trust me."

That was the only wake-up call I needed.

From that point on, I knew that every move I made had to be calculated. Every conversation, every glance, it all mattered. And it wasn't only about keeping my head low—it was about keeping myself protected from everyone around me. It's a game of survival, and that lesson, that one piece of advice, was enough to make me realize how serious it all was. But that guy was a good guy. And there were lots of good guys in there. Yet I needed to step carefully around them too.

Some of those people may never make it out of prison, but that didn't stop them from looking out for me. In a place like that, you've got to have each other's back. They gave me things that the system didn't give me: food, clothes, a toothbrush, all that little stuff that most people take for granted on the outside. A whole care package, just because. It wasn't much, but it meant the world. That's the thing you realize after a while in there—if you find the right people, they'll treat you like family, even when the world outside forgets about you.

Now, I won't sugarcoat it—prison is rough. You're constantly on edge, constantly looking behind you. But honestly, it's more of a mental game than anything. The hardest part is all the stuff you can't control. But if you stay out of people's way, keep your head down, and follow the rules, it's easier to get by. And by rules, I don't mean just the official ones. I mean the unwritten ones—the ones that the whole prison runs on. It's all about respect. If you don't respect people, you're going to find yourself in serious trouble. Simple things like not cutting in line, not putting your feet up on the table, not touching other people's things—it's that kind of behavior that can make or break your time inside.

And the consequences for breaking those rules? They're steep. You could lose your life for cutting in line. I've seen heads cracked open over less than that.

I was never one to make those mistakes. Maybe that's where not being able to read helped me out in that way. See, when you can't read, you learn to observe. You learn to pay attention to what's going on around you and to mirror what you see. It became my survival tactic. In prison, everything is about watching people—seeing how they move, how they act, what they do and don't do.

People passed the time all different ways, some of them acting no different than they would outside, hustling and whatnot. But a lot of people spent their days getting fit and . . . reading. Books. And letters from home.

It's lonely in prison, but even more so when all you have is a few minutes on the phone with whoever will talk to you at your assigned time. Guys read letters from the outside over and over. I couldn't do that. Guys were reading books—escaping from prison! In a way. But I couldn't do that yet, either.

I couldn't read yet, but I sure as hell kept working out, whenever I could. And I stayed out of people's way. I followed the rules. It worked. People started calling me "Youngster." It was a nickname that stuck. They'd say, "There goes Youngster, always working out." It wasn't about the nickname. It was about the respect that came with it. You give respect in prison, you'll find you're going to receive it too. It was a signal that I was part of the crew.

There were days when I'd feel cold, or sick, or just plain tired. But it didn't matter. I had to stick to the routine. When you're in a place like that, there's a certain way you have to live, and that routine becomes your anchor. People expect you to follow it, to stay disciplined. It's an unspoken rule. And when you're a part of a community like that, you don't want to let anyone down. You gotta stay consistent. I learned that real quick.

When I think about my time in prison now, sometimes I find myself even missing it. Not the bad parts—the violence, the isolation, the loneliness—but the simplicity of it. There was something kind of peaceful about it, in a strange way. Everything was laid out for you. You didn't have to worry about anything except doing your time and staying out of trouble. You went into every day knowing exactly what to expect. There was no guesswork. You didn't have to worry about bills, making decisions, all the complicated stuff that we deal with on the outside. It was stripped down to the basics. It wasn't freedom, but in some ways, it was a relief.

And for me, someone with OCD, that structure was even more of a relief. Everything in prison is predictable. There's a routine, a schedule. You know when you're eating, when you're exercising, when you're going to bed. Out here, on the outside, it's not like that. You need to make your own routine, and sometimes, it's hard to stick to it. Life gets messy, and it's harder to keep things in order. But in prison? It's almost like the routine keeps you grounded.

Since I've been out, I've had a lot of time to think about what prison taught me.

I didn't know how to integrate back into society when I was finally released. I was worried about how I was going to take care of myself. Toward the end of my sentence, I had been having a lot of mental struggles. I kept thinking I wasn't going to make it out, or that I was going to get in trouble again somehow, or something I'd forgotten was going to come back to bite me.

But I *did* make it out. I did. No matter how sure I was that I wouldn't, I did.

And here I am, today. Living a drastically different life, on my way to bigger and better things.

Which leads us to *Holes* by Louis Sachar.

When I read *Holes*, it hit me in a way I didn't expect. Maybe it was because I'd been through something like the main character, fourteen-year-old Stanley Yelnats, who was sentenced to a juvenile correctional facility in the desert called Camp Green Lake, where he was forced to dig holes. I, too, was sent away, thrown into a place where I was merely another body in a system that didn't care about me. Maybe it was because, like Stanley, I didn't even fully understand how I ended up there. But the biggest thing that stood out to me was this: When you're in a place like that, you don't just dig holes in the ground. You dig them in your mind. You sit there, alone with your thoughts, digging deeper into yourself: into your regrets, into your past, trying to figure out if you were ever meant to be anything more.

Prison isn't much different from Camp Green Lake. It's a place built to break you down, to strip you of your identity, to make you nothing but a number. The less individual you are, the easier you are to herd. Just like those boys at camp had to learn how to dig holes without killing themselves in the heat, I had to learn how to exist in prison without getting caught up in something worse.

And like Stanley, I was there because of something I barely understood at the time. Stanley's great-great-grandfather had been cursed a century ago. Bad luck ran in his family, and Stanley ended up serving time for something he didn't even do. That's exactly how I felt. I didn't grow up with generational wealth; I grew up with generational struggle. My ancestors made choices that somehow landed me in a bad neighborhood with a mom too busy and stressed to read me bedtime stories.

My whole life felt like I was carrying the weight of a curse I'd never asked for. From the moment I was born into the world, my fate had been written in some ways. The system already had assigned a place for me. A slot open, a cot waiting. All it took was the wrong opportunity at the wrong time, and suddenly, I was there.

And when I got there, as is the case in *Holes*, I realized the system didn't care if I was guilty or innocent. It didn't care about my story. It wasn't about justice; it was all about control. About making me do my time, breaking me down, making me feel like I wasn't worth anything. Those boys in *Holes* were digging because the Warden was looking for treasure, but they were told it was to "build character." That's exactly how they sell prison to you. They tell you it's about rehabilitation, about paying your debt to society. But when you're inside, you see the truth. It's not about making you better. It's about keeping you there, keeping you under control, making sure you don't think you can be more than what they say you are. Much like in the special ed classroom, you're less of a nuisance, a disturbance, if you're hidden away.

Holes was filled with characters that reminded me of the guys I met inside. There was X-Ray, who knew how to work the system and all its ins and outs better than anyone else and had his own way of surviving. There were guys like that in prison, too—those who weren't necessarily bad people but had been in long enough to know how to play the game. The ones who told me early on, "Don't trust nobody, don't talk too much, don't get involved in things that aren't your business." And then there was Zero—the quiet one, the one everyone underestimated, the one people thought wasn't smart because he didn't talk much and he couldn't read or write. But Zero was the smartest one there. He figured things out. He learned. He had potential nobody saw because they never looked.

That's how I felt. Like Zero. Like someone people had written off before they even knew me. The guards, the system, even some of the inmates—they saw me as just another body. Just another Youngster doing his time. But what they didn't know was that, like Zero, I wasn't about to stay that way. I wasn't going to let them bury me in that place and leave me there.

And then, in the book, something changes. Zero escapes and Stanley goes after him. They climb Big Thumb, the nearby mountain, and they survive together. They help each other, and that's what saves them. And that's real. Because in prison, the only thing that gets you through is the people. The good ones. The ones who look out for you. Those who give you a toothbrush when you don't have one, who tell you how things work so you don't make a mistake that could get you killed. There are people like that everywhere, even in the darkest places.

In *Holes*, the truth comes out. The Warden is exposed. The system gets called out for what it really is. But in real life, that doesn't always happen. In real life, the Wardens keep winning. The system keeps rolling on. But that doesn't mean you can't escape—not in the literal sense, but in the way that matters. You can still climb your own Big Thumb. You can still find your way out.

For me, reading would become that mountain. Every book I picked up was another step higher, another breath of fresh air, another glimpse of a future that didn't involve being buried alive in the system.

That's why *Holes* stuck with me when I eventually found it. Because I knew what it was like to dig. To spend every day working through the dirt, through the weight of everything trying to hold me there. But most importantly? I knew what it was like to find my way out.

And that's the thing people need to understand. Whether you're in prison, in poverty, in a bad situation that feels like it has no exit—there's always a way out. There's always something that can change everything. For me, it was reading. For Stanley and Zero, it was each other. But no matter what it is, you must believe in it before it finds you. You must start digging in the right direction.

Because if you dig long enough, eventually you're going to hit something real. Something priceless.

4

READING IS HELP ALONG THE WAY

Dirty Laundry: Why Adults with ADHD Are So Ashamed and What We Can Do to Help (2023), by Richard Pink and Roxanne Emery

Let me tell you a bit about what it's like being a person who can't read. And on top of it, what it's like to have been diagnosed with OCD, ADHD, and, once I went to prison, PTSD.

When I was young, I wanted to play video games. No big surprise, right? That's something that kids my age were always doing. Still are. But not everyone realizes that you need to be able to read to play. It's not the completely mindless activity critics would have you believe. You must read dialogue, item descriptions, maps, instructions, and so much more. Board games too! You've got rules, cards with information on them, spots on the board with text . . . and I couldn't read those things. Monopoly? A nightmare. I know a lot of people feel that way, but for me? Hell no.

If, say, a whole bunch of us were hanging out at a friend's place, and they wanted to play a game, not only could I not participate, but I also couldn't tell them why, either. I hid my illiteracy with everything I had. Being a teenager is hard enough without everybody knowing you can't read.

So I'd have to cause an issue. Not for attention, like when I was in school. In fact, it was kind of the opposite. I would try to throw people off so they wouldn't look too closely at me.

It could be anything. I might've made a personal problem of some kind, started a fight, for example. I'd say, "I don't wanna be here because this is boring," even though it wasn't. But I just didn't know how to communicate! I'd make a scene, get everybody focused on the fact that I was causing a ruckus. And as a result, I conflicted with the people around me, the people I called friends, *and* with myself.

And hey, it wasn't conscious. It wasn't like I thought, *Yeah, you know what's more fun than a board game? Strife and arguing, man, that'll be a great alternative.*

No, 'cause I didn't wanna be doing that! I wanted to do what the other kids were doing! I wish I could have said, "I can't read, and I don't want to play this because I'm going to struggle." Or asked for help. Something. But I couldn't. Or at least, I didn't think I could. I got defensive and threw out smoke and mirrors.

I would get so mad at myself. Shame, blame, and my ADHD/OCD go together hand in hand. OCD is about saying *if this or else this* or *if this, then this*. Everyone knows the common compulsion with light switches that many people with OCD often struggle with—they're compelled to flick the switches on and off a certain number of times before they leave the house or else . . . something bad will happen. That's up to the person. So it's a pretty easy walk to blame—something goes wrong, and, as a person with OCD, you think, *That's my fault because I didn't* . . . whatever the thing is. And this was amplified in prison, where I heard so many dudes sitting around saying, *If I had done this or hadn't done this, I wouldn't be here.* Like the butterfly effect.

ADHD made it so I couldn't pay attention. Even if someone was explaining game rules to me, suddenly I was lost. Again, I know that's a relatable thing for a lot of people—who doesn't zone out after the fifth rule about dice rolls? But for me, even the simple stuff would go over my head. As I couldn't read the rules or cards, or whatever, I'd spiral into these terrible cycles of self-blame. And that made me angry.

Defensive. Frustrated. Mean. Humiliated. Not a great party guest. Not a *joy to have in class*, again.

So every time someone wanted to play a board game, go to a restaurant and read the menu, make travel plans, or write someone a note on a holiday or birthday card, I couldn't do it. I must have seemed so difficult and picky, but honestly, I was terrified of being set up to fail in front of the people I cared about. It was embarrassing.

Sometimes I would give a friend a birthday card, but I never wrote in them. I would pick one with a cake or balloons on it. I probably gave my twenty-five-year-old friends cards meant for kids, but I didn't even know.

I could barely write my own name, so signing things was also pretty impossible. And then on top of it, I hated my handwriting so much that, even though I could spell my name, I hated to do it. I didn't learn any kind of signature until I was twenty-one. Someone told me that you just make your signature up, that there aren't clear rules about it. I thought it had to be cursive; and when I saw those crazy doctor's handwritten signatures, I thought everyone could read them perfectly but me. I didn't know that they were basically complicated squiggles and not necessarily meant to be legible.

I made up my own scribble, and that's when I started to sign cards. Just sign them.

As for day-to-day life, I could get by on a lot without too much trouble—such as doing laundry and making simple meals—but into adulthood I couldn't even, like, go to the grocery store. I couldn't buy ingredients to cook a specific dish, and it's not like I could read a recipe anyway. And because I couldn't read, I also didn't understand measurements. You can't even make Kraft Mac & Cheese if you can't read the instructions. I had to be shown how, then memorize it.

Even today, if my partner sends me to the grocery store, it takes me forever and I'm basically at the hip of every employee asking for help along the way. Still, too often, I'll do something like come home with apple cider vinegar instead of apple cider. It's embarrassing, man. Frustrating for everyone.

I've had to eat what other people made me, or whatever I could easily prepare. You wouldn't think of reading as being a necessary part of a balanced diet, but there it is!

Where I grew up, you need a car to get around. It's not a walkable city where you can get by without transportation. I took and failed the driver's test a few times, but eventually I was able to get the written portion down. I couldn't read at all, though, remember, so I had to take it in audio format. I still failed it and failed it. I had to print out the test at home and have my sister go through it with me to help me get over the threshold, 80 percent or whatever it was. By the time I passed, I had basically memorized the right and wrong answers. And it *is* still a manner of learning—I didn't forget what a yield sign looks like or means.

Not being able to read meant that while driving, I also couldn't read road signs. I basically had to memorize how to get from one place to another the old-fashioned way. I knew what a stop sign looked like, so I knew when to stop. But I couldn't follow any kind of directions. Couldn't read a GPS, either. I used to follow the little car on the screen to the best of my ability, but that wasn't always enough.

If you're a lifelong reader, you probably don't even think about it when the GPS tells you where to go. I can't keep an eye out for Exit 6, Market Street, for example, so I had to try and go diagonal when the little animated car did. I'd always miss exits. I still do. Honestly, even now, driving is scary because I have to do so many things at once. Reading doesn't feel like a passive skill to me, like I think it does for other people. It's a slow process. It's a *lot* of work.

I know I've mentioned this before, but I can't say it too much—you've got to trust people when you can't read. You're basically forced to ask for help, and hope that the help people give you is real. Trust doesn't come easily for all of us. That's part of why I leaned so heavily on romantic partners. You know (ideally) that you can trust them. And also? You have to *know* how to ask for help. You can't just get pissed off and stomp around—that won't get you help. You can't hide the fact that you *need* help. You must be able to say, *Hey, I want to make some mac and cheese, but I can't read the side of the box.* Otherwise, how will you let someone know that you're lost?

When you're illiterate, it's not only that you are kept behind in not knowing how to read, it also affects how your brain is shaped for society. When you can't pursue a lead to follow a dream, or can't look something up and learn, the world seems entirely inaccessible. The way to access most information is by reading, and without that, in life, what you see is what you get.

You know how you might wonder something, be it *who was that actor in that movie* or *how to put out a grease fire*? You Google it, right? Then read the results. I can't do that. You might think, *Well, you can watch a YouTube video instead.* But not if I can't even type out the question. No, I'll never find out it was Jason Statham, and I'll watch my kitchen go up in flames instead. Using something like Siri can work too, but it doesn't replace the ability to get fuller answers, to double-check the information,

Not being able to read limits so much important background. It's not simply that I didn't get to know what the deal was with Jay Gatsby. It's everywhere. The back of a pill bottle, the road signs, the directory at a mall. But also, it limited my ability to learn *new* things. I was lost with numbers too. I couldn't learn in school—not about history, science, nothing. The framework we're in matters. How we got to where we are: politically, socially, culturally. Math is money. Science is medicine. I'm missing all that. And if I want to know something, I gotta ask someone. I can't easily explore stuff on my own. So if the person I ask even knows the answer, it might be heavily biased.

It also means that I have a different framework from the rest of the people I meet. And if they come from a totally different background, I have trouble relating, because I don't have enough information. For me, as someone who couldn't read, it meant that people outside of my own world, my own routine, were more than strangers.

Reading is information, and information is famously power. Reading affects behavior, emotions, and decision-making too. Even though it's not the only contributing factor, reading is the *running on a treadmill* of mental health. Exercise. It keeps your brain in good shape. I didn't understand that for a long time. Reading is a way to actively use your brain to find new worlds, other experiences, and to put yourself somewhere you haven't been. And slowly you start to recognize yourself in strangers too. To find yourself in characters you thought you had nothing in common with. To relate. To break patterns and assumptions and see the world isn't only you, it's actually infinite—that kind of freedom can have a massive impact. It makes you realize that what you thought you had to live with isn't all there is.

Like, if someone reads a story about people in a bad relationship, they might see themselves in it. They can see something about their own life. It's not the same as watching a movie, either, where you might look at the character and see so many differences. In reading, all the characters are played by your own mind. People who aren't accessing other people's stories assume *I'm broken, I like toxic relationships*, when they just don't know how to grow or choose with an open mind.

I got defensive about needing help early in life. Not that I realized why I was defensive—it was more like I felt defensive about who I was. Always trying to prove I had value. See, I felt like I had to. Always always always. And that was how I stayed: in the middle of the pack with a chip on my shoulder.

But I never led the pack, you know? I always lived in the shadow of someone else. I never found my own way, never *made* my own way. Instead, I mirrored and mimicked what the people around me were doing and being. And that felt a lot easier. I didn't have to do any work on myself. I didn't have to walk in the world as a person who doesn't know how to read, who has PTSD, who has OCD, who's been traumatized and grew up in a way I wasn't proud of. I couldn't tell people to meet me where I was. I tried to live like I was someone else. Usually, like whoever I hung out with.

And that was dangerous. If something was happening that I didn't think was right, or even if I wanted to be doing something else, I was too scared to tell my friends that. I was too afraid they'd make fun of me, or worse, that I'd lose friends. Losing friends, for me, was literally about life and death. I mean, I wouldn't be alive now if I hadn't gotten so much help.

I've never been alone. And I'm still afraid to be. I went from high school, living at my mom's house; to prison; and then back to my mom's. Then I met a girl and moved right in with her. I tried to mimic the world she brought me into. She was an amazing person, and she thought I was her Prince Charming. I wasn't. I was lying, mimicking. I was pulling her along, telling her nothing about my reality. She deserved to find her real Prince Charming. So, we broke up. And I went right into another relationship.

I was in that first relationship because I felt love. In hindsight, I see that it was also helpful that she could assist me with the things I wasn't confident about. I figured that's what the give and take of a relationship was. But I couldn't communicate those things either way. I was too scared to tell people how scared I was. But I can see now that there was a piece of my soul that needed something she had to give. And that makes me feel pretty guilty.

By now, I have learned to ask for help in ways that are as healthy as I know how to do it. The book that helped me with that was *Dirty Laundry: Why Adults with ADHD Are So Ashamed and What We Can Do to Help*, by Richard Pink and Roxanne Emery. I'm an adult with ADHD and illiteracy, and my life is a string of people who have helped me along the way.

This book dives into the complex and often painful feelings of shame that many adults with ADHD experience. Pink and Emery talk about how these feelings of shame can shape the lives of ADHD sufferers, and what we can do to help address and ease that burden. I think it ties in with the themes we've touched on in this chapter. For me personally, my ADHD has played a big role in perpetuating some of the unhealthy patterns I've mentioned. It's been a factor in the cycles I've struggled with, and I know I'm not alone in that.

There are a lot of people out there who, like me, have ADHD, and sometimes it can feel like a weight that's hard to shake off, especially if it wasn't diagnosed or properly supported during childhood. That ongoing struggle can be compounded by the shame that was instilled in them as children—shame for things they couldn't control or fully understand at the time. And it's so important to recognize that it's not their fault.

Kids with ADHD, just like all kids, need assistance, understanding, and guidance from the adults around them. But unfortunately, too often, support isn't available or isn't given in a way that makes sense. The reality is all children struggling with ADHD need that kind of support to thrive. Without it, it's easy to see how cycles of struggle can persist into adulthood.

Reading *Dirty Laundry* made it easier for me not only to accept help, but also to learn how to ask for it in a way that was clear to those around me. This book speaks to the importance of empathy for those with ADHD—not just kids, but adults as well.

Dirty Laundry is about how to help loved ones, but it helped me to help myself too. When I first heard about ADHD and OCD, I was wrong about what they truly mean. Illiteracy? I was worried people would make jokes or assume I was raised in the woods. But books like this teach empathy for those around us and *also* for ourselves.

5

READING IS LOVE

365 Quotes to Live Your Life By (2019), by I. C. Robledo

NOW, ASKING FOR HELP IS all well and good. And a lot of people out there—who need a hell of a lot less help than I do—struggle with asking for it when they need it.

Dating when you have extra needs can feel impossible. When I was younger, I did it without any self-awareness at all. What I'm about to go into is embarrassing for me and tough to admit, because I know I have a good heart—but for a while there, I wasn't a great guy. I didn't mean to have hurt anyone. I wasn't laughing about it behind the scenes. But I had little self-awareness, and I was trying like hell to survive, so the result ended up being that I was . . . let's just say, not at my best.

I have been a liar. A cheater. A manipulator.

Not out of a lack of respect for anyone. Not because it was fun. Or because I wanted to take advantage of people. But because I didn't have the tools to do things the right way, so I did what I could.

I couldn't study for the test on geography, so I got good at cheating. In a way, doing it the right way was the least of my concerns. When I was looking for a job, I'd date a girl who could spell and count and read, so she could help me job search. I looked for girls who naturally wanted to take care of others, banking on their kindness. This meant that my relationships, especially romantic ones, led to one familiar dynamic: If I get into a relationship with someone, and trust them with who I am, that means a lot more than it would for many people. My partner isn't just my friend or my romantic interest—she has to be my caregiver too.

When I was in high school, it was a bit simpler. My girlfriends typically helped me out with schoolwork. I was still living at home, not having to worry about bills and that kind of thing yet. But eventually, my whole life would become something I needed help with.

Appointments. Hanging out with people. Navigating to places. Cooking. Figuring out why the TV wasn't working. Filling out forms at the doctor's office. Reading warning labels on medicine. Before I started learning to read, I was at the mercy of whoever would help me. And who do you spend the most time with? Your partner.

So, this limits the kinds of dynamics and relationships you can even have. You look for somebody who is a natural caretaker. Someone who wants that. The problem is that those caretaker traits are not always healthy: They might be the result of an earlier trauma—the person may struggle with codependency. Or maybe they can't help but feel beholden to the people who ask them for help. Perhaps that person doesn't know how to look out for themselves, to prioritize their own mental health. Sometimes, that leads to resentment on both sides.

So I looked for girls who would be there for all that.

Kinda puts the whole attraction/chemistry/love thing on the back burner. Not to mention the added challenges that came with being with me at that time. I was so defensive that it would often lead to fights.

Because let's not forget, either, that my personality was built on top of my limitations. I ended up being protective of myself because of them. If I had to tell someone that I couldn't read—or, that I can't read that *well*, now—I'm making myself vulnerable. I'm always afraid of what the response is gonna be. Usually, it's nice. Usually. But sometimes, someone will be like *that's not my problem*. That's when I get edgy, that's when I go into *fight-or-flight* a little bit. Hard not to feel the avalanche of all my excuses and explanations every time someone makes me feel bad about it.

And then there is the question that always comes up early in relationships: Are we right for each other? I couldn't simply ask myself that. It would be like taking off a life vest in the middle of the ocean.

The question instead became not just *How can I live without her?* but *How can I live without her help? No, seriously, how?*

That puts a heavy weight on a relationship. All the weight of *me*. It's not my goal to be someone else's problem—I should be a bonus, right? Relationships should add value. I need to bring half the party to the table. I want someone to be with me because they love me, and I want to be with someone because I love them. Not be together out of fear or obligation. On either side.

That's the thing: Not only was I worried that I was with people for the wrong reason, but I was also worried they felt too guilty to leave. And if you've ever been in a relationship, you probably know the effect worry and paranoia can have. They cause problems that wouldn't ordinarily even exist.

Whether I liked it or not, I was *using* people. I felt like I didn't have a choice, and in some ways, I didn't. I wasn't able to stand on my own two feet, and to some extent, I'm still not. I stayed in relationships with people that I probably wouldn't have otherwise, only because they were able to help me do some rudimentary tasks. I wasn't being honest, with them or myself. I made decisions based on what a person could do for me, and not solely on who they were.

And that was awful. It felt awful. I feel bad about it still. Nobody wants to be used; nobody wants attention for what they can do and nothing else. It's humiliating to require so much of someone else. And at what point would I know if someone was staying with me out of guilt? Did we truly love each other?

I don't feel good about this situation. And every day, I wake up and try to fix it in some way. But, again, you can't fix something like this overnight. I know I still come with extra baggage for those who love me. Even though I've come a long way, I still have more needs than the average person. And I want to get better.

To find a healthy romantic relationship, someone like me has to look for a partner who has done enough work on themselves to not fall victim to codependency, but who still wants to take care of you in some way. And that can be hard to identify correctly and hard to trust, let alone find.

Whew. This is all pretty tough to say out loud. It's the first time I've actually said a lot of this stuff to anyone else. Most of it, really. It's not like I have much of a history of confiding in people.

It wasn't until I met Anne that I began opening up.

When I met her, I was in a growing process in my life. It was the first time I was learning while going into a relationship. I was learning how to be a man. I was learning how to grow up; how to be honest. How to be truthful. How to love. I was learning how to see somebody other than looking at myself. How to be less selfish. How to accept love. I knew I was deserving of love, but I was also in a place in life where I wasn't sure who *I* was. Anne was helping me see a lot that I didn't know was there. She's a very patient person when it comes to letting people try to figure themselves out, so she was very accepting of me just being, you know, who I was. I had OCD, ADHD, PTSD, and I was still drinking at the time. I was still into some bad habits.

But I looked at her, she looked at me, and she saw *me*. For whatever reason, we trusted each other. She didn't make any instant judgments, and that was new to me. She wanted me to prove myself.

The fact that she trusted me made me want to earn her trust. And plus, she was honest with me. I believed I was hearing what she honestly thought. She was giving and caring, but she took care of herself too.

Since I was being more honest with her, I had the chance, for the first time, to hear that I wasn't alone. There was a lot about my experience that was familiar to her, even though we had very different lives.

Also, Anne was already a mom. So I got to see what a good person she was with her child. And you know how moms are—they're strong. And for the first time, I saw how a mom could treat her kid, given enough space to do it. It was an eye-opener to see her with her own little boy and witness the love and care she gave him. She wasn't perfect—no one is—but I could see how it was supposed to be.

We were better together. She made me better, for sure. We went vegan; we took care of ourselves. We built a strong foundation.

Anne. In many ways, she's the real hero of my story. My partner, the mother of my children, the spark that lit the match that started my reading fire.

The whole reason I wanted to learn to read is that Anne gave me a book of quotes for Christmas in 2020.

365 Quotes to Live Your Life By, by I. C. Robledo. I used to go over to Anne's house with YouTube videos of motivational speakers I liked. Speakers who stirred me to join their ranks. I'd watch them and get so excited by the stuff they were saying that I couldn't wait to share it with her. That felt like the beginning of something. The absorbing and then sharing of information.

It sounds crazy now—this woman who liked me calling me over for us to have a good time, and me over here showing her motivational-speaking videos. She was like, *Let's hang out and have fun*, and I was like, *Okay, but let's watch this TED Talk super quick.*

But she was, and still is, such a big part of what made me want to expand my mind like that. Trust me, she inspires a lot of thoughts and feelings, but I was so determined on my path at that time that all I could focus on was my end goal. Above *everything.* Even if a beautiful woman was sitting right there, I was hungry for an education I'd been starved of.

Motivational Speeches and Chill just doesn't have quite that catchy a ring to it.

But her buying the quote book for me came from that experience, and from her desire to give me an outlet for my passion. She saw how much I needed it and could tell that I needed it in a way that was easy to digest. She knew that I couldn't read well, though the extent to which I couldn't and the limitations it caused would be something that came out later, over more time.

For me that book connected with my passion. I thought: *Whoa, I can take what I learn and share it.* I *could be one of those people standing on a stage, sharing their vulnerabilities with the world.* And eventually, *Hey, I can change my life.* Those were my dreams. Why wasn't I doing everything I could to make them happen?

Before Anne, I didn't know what I was capable of because nobody had made anything feel real to me yet. But this woman gave me patience and saw my needs—and she didn't just assist me but brought me new ideas. Not just helping me read the side of the cold medicine bottle but bringing a book into my life with the intention of it bringing me more life. Not for surviving. For thriving.

Anne didn't just see what I didn't have. She saw what I might have. She didn't just see what I couldn't do. She saw what I might, one day, be able to do.

Not only were the quotes short and easy to work through, but each was like an open door to a new perspective. Anne didn't just give me a new room to walk into, she gave me a new galaxy. Limitless.

And all because she believed in me.

While growing my mind with the things I learned from my quote book, *Quotey* (that's what I called it—or, as I think of it, that's what I named him), I found some quotes that scared me. Like I said before, I was afraid of change. Afraid of accepting a spiritual world. Once you become a reader and begin to learn, you start to realize that the spiritual world is an open gateway to a higher knowledge for all human existence.

Now, how we view that world is up to us. You can do God, you can do Buddha, you can call it the Universe—there are all sorts—but deep down, they all have the same basis. As I tapped into this wider consciousness, reading began to feel like I was turning around in my own brain, literally. Like I was flipping my eyes backward and seeing that there was a whole other world—an even bigger one—living in my mind.

It did something to me, man. It was a sudden, massive realization. And it changed me.

Kinda like a near-death experience. It does something to you, right? It pushes you somewhere beyond your level of consciousness. It changes your vocabulary about things you know because you have faced the unknown. It speaks to you in a way that's outside of your comprehension. It shocks the system.

You can see this in the way you think about time, during or after a traumatic event. Once you've gathered your bearings, you might realize that the event was only ten seconds long. Although logically this makes sense, emotionally it might feel like it was a two-hour experience. That little bit of space that's unexplainable to anyone who hasn't gone through it. A car crash happens in an instant, but people aren't kidding when they say it feels like time slows down. I've experienced it myself. I remember having that feeling of infinity creeping up behind me. It's a spiritual middle spot where you're experiencing *and* reflecting on the present moment as it happens.

But what about a traumatic event that isn't sudden, but which takes place over a long time? It's slow, but so earth-shattering that it changes your life forever after. I didn't feel drastically different, but I knew: Something was changing inside me. Like stamina or lung capacity increases after a few weeks of jogging—it doesn't suddenly make you Usain Bolt, but it's clear that your breaths are getting deeper. The possibilities feel within reach.

And in a weird way, the quotes I read in *Quotey*—a huge collection of quotes from a wide variety of people, organized by themes such as how to focus on what you *can* control, and how to focus on positivity instead of negativity—could apply to just about anything in *this* book. More to the point, they could apply to anything in life. I chose to use *Quotey* for this chapter because that book has covered me from the beginning of my reading journey to now, where the road continues.

6

READING IS WILD

Charlotte's Web (1952), by E. B. White,
with illustrations by Garth Williams

I HAD NO IDEA THAT THE QUOTE BOOK Anne had given me would start me on a long, winding path, and eventually lead me to my own kingdom of knowledge.

The unlikely kindling for this small fire in me was COVID. That's the honest truth. The pandemic affected everyone differently. Lots of people suffered terrible losses—of their loved ones or of their own long-term health. People who had woken up every day for years and gone to work were suddenly slowing down, staying home. People who hadn't had time for their families were now with them constantly. Normal things like going to the grocery store were either forbidden or completely different experiences. And for once, we all had something in common—we were scared, we didn't know what was coming next, and we were looking for answers from the people who were supposed to help us.

In a way, this was how I'd lived my life. Uncertainty, a great deal of fear, and dependence. Of course, the pandemic also blew up my own carefully constructed existence, where I had figured out how to get by.

Under everything, every single day, there was a sense of panic without a hint of a solution in sight. And further beneath even all *that* was the sudden realization that things can change completely, forever, overnight, and your fragile house of cards *can* collapse.

So, yeah, while I sat in my house for weeks and months on end like everyone else did, watching the news for some kind of miracle cure or announcement that it was all over and we could go back to our normal lives, an extra layer of dread was settling right in the pit of my stomach.

I didn't know how to take care of myself. I wasn't *able* to take care of myself. The sign in front of the eggs at the grocery store might have said customers could only buy one dozen per trip or it might have said there was a chance they were infected with the coronavirus, and there was no way I'd know the difference. This had always been true, but now I was finding that even the unstable world I'd grown used to could be turned inside out.

That opened my eyes to the fact that I was drowning. I was completely dependent upon having someone close by to be my life vest. And if the world changed any more, I was going to be left even farther behind all the people I knew and loved. And everyone else too.

All the systems I had in place stopped working. I'm not somebody who is super comfortable with change, and once it was pushed on me like that, it was sink or swim, and I knew I had to change along with it.

And change was overdue.

After prison, I had become a fitness instructor. Physicality was one of the few things I felt in control of. I was always good at sports, so it was the easy thing. I started doing videos online, as it was a way to use what I'd learned in my speech class—speaking out loud could connect me to others. And I didn't have to read. Just speak.

Words without my usual barriers. I could communicate with words! Something I was desperate to do. I craved the expression. But I could feel there was something empty in what I was doing. Plus, the way some people go to college—like I had wanted to—and come out feeling more qualified for something, that's kinda how I felt after prison. I had been hyper-focused on the only thing I had to do, which was take care of my mind (as best I could) and my body. I was in amazing shape, the way you only can be after spending hours a day doing push-ups, pull-ups, crunches, and walking around for miles in a small space.

During COVID, there wasn't a lot of personal training going on. I did TikTok just to keep putting stuff out there, keep working with people. It was okay, nothing went viral or anything. I was putting myself out there. Sharing, even if it was only showing people how you could work out in your apartment.

But at the same time, I was starting to read.

Remember how I said Anne had given me a galaxy when she gave me *Quotey*? Well, she did. But it felt like in a space movie where you get pushed out of the ship and you're floating out there, with no way to get back.

And what I was seeing, what I was learning, *the fact that I was learning*, was as terrifying as it was exciting.

It felt like magic, different parts of my brain were lighting up. And they literally were. I had known about the here and now, I had known not to go down this street or talk to that dude or to take my eyes off the road. Things to keep me alive. But now I was getting ideas. Ideas that weren't my own. And I had to decide what I believed. What was the difference between reading someone's theory on something and thinking about it myself? Both came through in my own voice in my mind.

I began to feel crazy. I mean it. Like I was hearing voices. And I was. And they weren't mine.

And then, as I read, I could hear this little voice in my head sounding out the words and turning them into something I could understand. As this happened, I became aware of the voice in my head. Was I actually hearing it? Or was I imagining it? What was the difference? It scared me. I didn't trust myself. Had this voice lived in there all along?

What *was* it? It felt like a psychotic break. Like constantly having someone standing behind me whispering new ideas. Didn't matter how good the ideas were—who wants some stranger standing behind them, saying shit?

I had never felt anything like it, and in that very moment, I snapped. I thought I was going crazy.

Do you remember that little guy in *Men in Black*, the tiny alien operating the robot-human's body from inside the robot's head? I felt like him, suddenly. Kids ask a lot of questions, but something they're also very good at is accepting reality without asking too many questions. Adults struggle more with things that break the rules of their world. I was learning, all at once, about what it feels like to be a conscious reader. It's like, in my thirties, I was suddenly given a sense of smell or hearing. I got a whole new perspective on beliefs I'd taken for granted my entire life. It was a total shock to my system.

I started challenging things that I'd never even thought about before. Like, for example, I'm Black. Nothing crazy about that, right? But I got all tripped out because I'm . . . well, I'm not Black! My skin is brown. And suddenly, I realized that I'd never questioned that. It was just another thing that made me feel crazy. I would go up to people and ask them what color I was. They'd all say I was Black. So, I wasn't crazy. Right?

OCD thoughts tend to follow an *if this, then this* meter. Man, that was happening to me all over the place. If I'm not Black, then what am I? If I'm brown, then what does that mean? Every new revelation led to an existential crisis.

Everything in my brain was shifting. All the superstitions I'd grown up with. I always stopped in my tracks when a black cat crossed my path. But now, I was like, "Shit, what if you just . . . don't believe that?"

I was questioning my OCD superstitions too. The *if I don't stay in the car another hour before getting out, someone in my life will die* thought process was being interrupted by the fact that *known* things were no longer known. So, if the OCD thought wasn't true, then . . . what? And what did it mean that I had such strange ideas to begin with?

Thoughts like these really messed with me. They filled my head and were louder than anything else in a way. It was rough. I wasn't sure how to let go of everything I needed to, and I wasn't even sure which things needed to go.

It was too much for me to handle. I didn't have a teacher or anybody around to explain this to me, someone to drip it to me in doses that I could readily digest. I didn't have a foundation. It was only me reading my books and thinking. And it took me a long time to finally comprehend the quotes I read from *Quotey*. Because the technical mechanics of reading are different from reading comprehension.

Knowing words isn't the same as understanding them. And I was starting to get them. They began sitting with me in moments when I didn't want them to. Like, why was one group of quotes in *Quotey* aligned with one particular message? And why was that message different from the other messages? And why does this quote remind me of this moment from my past? Why does that one make me feel bad?

It was painful. I became more frightened by the day. So, I thought, *I am going insane.*

I mean, having grown up with OCD, I used to do so many things—switch off that light switch or someone dies, close that drawer, don't step on the sidewalk cracks—all without thinking. But now, reading had opened my mind enough that I could observe myself doing these actions, and they seemed . . . crazy!

I was in the basement, going through my thoughts. That's when this happened. There was a war in my mind. The new knowledge was trying to fight for space with the old knowledge. And I felt like I was just watching. All the things I took for granted suddenly seemed weird. Why do we wear shoes or put a tree up at the holidays? Why anything?

What *is* anything? What is . . . *what?*

I told my partner, "Hey, I need to go to the hospital!"

"What? Why?" She obviously thought I looked fine, so what was I talking about?

"I don't feel right. I'm hearing things and having crazy thoughts."

"You're fine, just calm down—"

"I'm *not!* Trust me, I'm not."

She didn't argue then. I don't think she knew the extent of what I was experiencing. I think she was observing it, like: *Damn, dude, you're going through some major shifts, huh?*

But she went with me to the emergency room. She was trying to make me feel better the whole time, but I couldn't accept it. I needed the doctors to tell me. I believed that doctors could fix anything. That's one of those kid beliefs. But she knew that wasn't the case.

She told me, "Oliver, this is something you're going to have to face."

"I don't even know what *it* is."

"This is your brain on books. Everything's new to you now. It's all good but tough, I know, but there's no magic pill. This is a battle you're going to have to go inside and fight on your own."

She told me that the doctors would give me recommendations for some kinds of help, but it might be help that I didn't want or wouldn't take. Like going to a psych hospital, being observed for seventy-two hours. Then what? I wanted that magic pill that Anne pointed out didn't exist.

"They're only going to look at you as someone who's gonna need medication or something," she told me. "They're not going to understand that your brain is evolving. You're changing. You're technically in a position that might look a little crazy, but I don't think you are."

She was right. My brain was broken open. I had gone from zero to a hundred in no time flat, and it was terrifying. Suddenly, I realized, it felt like nothing could break my worldview, because the new worldview was open enough to account for whatever happened. If an alien had landed on my roof, I don't even think I'd have been surprised. If I saw them, all big and green walking around the White House lawn on TV, I'd be like, *Oh, that finally happened, like Ray Bradbury predicted* and change the channel. Suddenly, everything felt possible.

And that was petrifying.

Humans aren't supposed to live without some kind of rule set. Limitations tell us where we are. I'm standing on the ground because gravity pushes me down, right? I can only jump so high and move so fast, and most people have similar limitations, so we build doors, stairs, buses, cars, and planes to work around those limitations. We have a lot of similar limitations when it comes to the mind and heart. We fall in love, we fall out of love, we think one thing, we think another. We all have these shared rules.

But what if those rules just went away?

If I can use this new perspective to rid myself of some old beliefs that aren't serving me, what happens if I choose wrong? What if I lose a belief that *is* serving me? What if I accidentally throw out the part of me that doesn't want to hurt the people I love? Will I still be in control? Will I still be me?

Power is scary. And I'd just gotten access to a very potent source.

And, no matter how much help I asked for, I was still going to have to face some parts of it entirely alone. Entirely within my own mind. Some parts of that process were going to be painful, and some of them were going to hurt the people around me, if I wasn't careful.

Nobody's beliefs are necessarily all right or wrong. We can't prove anything to each other unless it's a science experiment. The thing that's so crazy about being an adult who comes to this place with reading and thinking is that you kind of know you're going to have to choose some things to believe. And you wonder how much say you're going to get in the matter.

When I think about all that chaos and argument that was going on in my head, and about going to the hospital like I did—when I'm trying to answer the question *Why did you end up going to the hospital?*—I only have one answer: *Who wouldn't?*

But I got relief there. And later, the new way I was thinking allowed me to explore things that had previously been too wild to envision. Things like making more money, being a better father, moving out of Bethlehem. I used to shut down when those thoughts occurred to me.

I was on the cusp of extraordinary change. I knew it too. There was no way to be in my mind and body at that time and not recognize that a transformation was taking place. When I read *Charlotte's Web*, a year or so later, I looked back on this time and saw my own story reflected in it.

Wilbur the pig begins as a naive and dependent character, like I was. My world, like his, had been small. Like Wilbur, I too hadn't previously questioned what was around me. Then, his friend, Charlotte the barn spider, writes messages in her web that quite literally save Wilbur. Wilbur was scared of change. I was too. It was overwhelming. And when he realizes Charlotte might not always be there to help, Wilbur is petrified. I had Anne, and I was so grateful to have her, but what if she left me? What if something terrible happened?

If . . . then. OCD thoughts were looping.

Maybe Anne was Charlotte, giving me the words that would save my life. I had a feeling they would. But I was learning that the process along the way would be profoundly difficult. In ways I never knew enough to imagine.

7

READING IS CHANGE

The Book of Jose: A Memoir (2022), by Fat Joe with Shaheem Reid

GROWING UP THE WAY I DID, I'd never truly had what you might call an identity shift. Most people, I guess, go through shifts like that when they leave for college, when they go through a big break-up, when they have kids, and about a dozen times a year in their teens. Not me, though. From where I sat, it looked like everyone else was always on their way somewhere new.

Since my childhood didn't have that same upward trajectory of constant learning and growth, I stayed sorta . . . stagnant. Not to mention, I didn't have the frame of reference to self-actualize. I couldn't think of myself as someone who could change, grow, pursue new horizons. Nobody else looked at me that way, so I couldn't either.

Reading gave me my first real experience with a word that I'd never had much reason to use before: *peace*.

Yeah, peace. I was beginning to find peace. I didn't recognize it at first. All I knew was that I would sit down for an hour or two and try to read. I wasn't connected to anything—no phone or computer, no friends to message or talk to. Just me, myself, and my book.

I was spending a lot of time on me, and I was totally into it. But I guess I wasn't quite ready to feel everything that came with this me time.

I was exposing myself to moods I'd never felt before. The chaos was shut out. I was focused, determined, and exploring. Picture a child who has only ever lived in a room filled with banging drums, clattering cymbals, and piano keys being banged ceaselessly for years. That kid would get used to sleeping in such chaos. But what would happen if all the noise suddenly stopped? I'm curious. Something surely would.

It's in this new world that I lost myself. My brain was alphabet soup. And I was already changing. My old life didn't seem to fit anymore.

At the time that I ended up in the hospital, I was still firmly held by the core belief system of the neighborhood I grew up in. But now, the people I had known but never been honest with were starting to make less sense to me. I couldn't just kick it and chill and not deal with these new perspectives that they weren't interested in. I don't know how many people I grew up with couldn't read. If any of them couldn't, they kept it to themselves—which I understand, of course—but I do know that I never saw any of my friends or family reading. Not once.

So, when I began reading, it was kind of embarrassing to bring that around the people I knew. Like, it wasn't on the table for me to go hang out with my old friends and be like "Hey, check out this book!" They might have accepted it, honestly; I have no way of knowing because I was way too insecure to find out. So I tried to go to them the same way I always had: to bring them the same parts of myself that I'd always brought—what they were used to—even though there was more to me now.

I realized that hanging out with them was taking time away from reading. And that's what I wanted to be doing. I felt like a kid with an alien hidden in his closet. I couldn't just go back to my old ways—I wanted to figure out what was up with the alien!

I was casting myself out farther onto that new ocean, watching the people onshore get smaller and smaller and eventually disappear.

But the thing is, it wasn't only them. Maybe this new feeling didn't have much to do with them at all. It was the old me. All the old versions of me, none of which I ever wanted to be again. I felt lonely from myself suddenly. My old patterns, routines, interests—everything was starting to feel a little off.

The Book of Jose is a memoir by rapper and actor Joseph Antonio Cartagena, known as Fat Joe, who grew up in the Bronx. Fat Joe was torn between the dangerous life he'd been used to—running the streets, stealing, selling drugs—and trying to make it in the rap business. He would be torn, because part of growing is, sometimes, becoming lonelier for a while. He could feel himself shifting to a different level of life; whenever he went back home, he wasn't the same Fat Joe that the people in his neighborhood knew. And he couldn't convince them that, under the layers of change, he was still in there. I had very similar experiences.

Boy, did that speak to me when I read *The Book of Jose* later on, when I was deeper into my reading journey. But when I did, I saw more clearly what I'd actually been dealing with at the end of my time in Pennsylvania.

I could tell I was becoming someone . . . new. Someone different. I was still Oliver, but I wasn't the *same* Oliver. Like I got bit by a vampire. I had new needs, and my new life kept me away from the old ways I was used to.

At the time, I had been running a fitness studio. I was given the space to use for free by a friend whom I used to train. I would train him and any of his friends, whomever he asked me to, and in exchange, I was allowed to use the space. I ran boot camps out of the studio, called Oliver's Firehouse Fitness. I built up a good clientele. I'll be honest, I still don't know how I did it to this day. I was just doing things. I ran around with signs. I printed out flyers. I needed help with both, of course. I talked to people on the streets. I was never completely serious about it, but I just did it and it worked.

But when COVID hit, my friend had to sell the building. He told me it was a good run, and he was impressed by what I'd done to build the place up. When he asked what I'd do next, I told him I wasn't sure. Maybe I'd save up for a van, move all my stuff into it, and be a mobile personal trainer. Go to people's houses and do fitness in their driveways. I didn't know.

The next day, he called me up and said, "Hey, man, as a token of my appreciation for everything you've done, I'm gonna buy you a van."

I mean, I was broke. I still don't know why he did it. But I was so grateful, and I took him up on it. I put all my equipment in the van and started doing what I said I would do. I can't believe the generosity of that guy, to this day. I thank him with all my heart.

It was becoming clear to me that I no longer had a reason to stay in Pennsylvania. Except for Anne, but what if she would come with me? Now that I had the van, I had a way to leave.

It wasn't long after I got out of the emergency room—after maybe a week of staying at home—that we did it. We went to Florida. It was 2020, nobody was driving anywhere. The roads were empty. So, I thought, *Let's go somewhere new.* My inside world was expanding, I wanted my outside world to get bigger too.

We didn't make a solid plan or anything. We only had a vague idea to go visit my brother, who lived in Florida. But after that trip, I decided I wanted to move there. Where usually I would have been like, *I gotta go home 'cause that's what I do, that's where I live*, now I was like . . . *Maybe I don't know where I live yet. Maybe I can change it. Chance it. Get out.*

A lifetime of obstacles, blocked lanes, and suddenly . . . I could fly.

I was about to move to Florida. I couldn't believe it.

And I was firm in it, I was sure it was happening. This was it. I was going to be gone and stay gone. My friends back home weren't the only ones who didn't recognize me anymore; I didn't even recognize *myself* anymore.

When I woke up one morning in South Florida, I got a call from an old friend, this guy I knew who had moved out to California with another friend of mine to do stunt bike riding. He randomly decided to Instagram video call me—the first time I'd ever gotten one—and I picked up.

Now, I didn't talk to these guys almost ever. Basically, the kinds of people you see once or twice a year, people you nod to in the grocery store. So, when they called, I thought, *What did I do? Is something wrong?*

But they were all hype when I got on the phone with them. It seemed like they had just gone through a shift of their own. They were like:

"Yo, what's up, man?"

"Nothing much, what's up?"

And we were just talking.

"You ever thought of moving to California, bro?"

Why would they ask me that? I'd never thought about leaving Pennsylvania before, and now, the moment that I do, everyone knows and someone's pitching me new ideas?

I was starting to believe in manifesting, even if I didn't have the language for it yet.

"I don't know, man, something just told me. I've seen a few of your Instagram videos, and we were talking, and your name came up, so I was like, huh, I'm gonna call him right now."

Turned out they had seen some videos about my mobile training van situation. We talked on and on about what was happening at home and all that. But then:

"I want to let you know, hey, if you ever want to move to California and do that business here, California is the mecca of doing things like that."

Mind you, I'm thinking about California like . . . Snoop Dogg, Dr. Dre, *Real Housewives*. I didn't know a thing about what it was like to live there. But it didn't sound like a place I had any reason to go. And I told him that.

"Man," he said, "that is not California. That's only what you see on TV."

I was in exactly the right headspace for that to resonate. I didn't know what I didn't know.

As soon as I got off the phone, he sent me a message and Anne helped me read it:

"Yo, man, I'm serious. If you want to come to California, come; you can stay with me until you get on your feet."

The whole place was all made up, in my mind. Not the kind of place I could actually *go* to. Everyone there was a character in a movie or a rap video. I had no idea you could just . . . be there, sitting on the beach on a random Monday.

But I was about to find out what it was like. Firsthand.

It reminded me again of *The Book of Jose.* Fat Joe had to leave behind the version of himself that no longer fit, the one that his old neighborhood still expected him to be. He didn't simply outgrow his past—he built something new, something bigger. He turned the loneliness of change into fuel, and in doing so, he became the kind of success that the old him couldn't have even imagined. Maybe I could too.

8

READING IS YOURS

You Owe You: Ignite Your Power, Your Purpose, and Your Why (2022), by Eric Thomas, PhD

Eric Thomas's *You Owe You: Ignite Your Power, Your Purpose, and Your Why*, is another motivational book, and to me, it is next-level. Even if you've never read it, just the title tells you so much of what you need to know. *You Owe You.* It's a book about *you.* It's about taking control of your own life, your own power, your own identity. What I was doing at this time was all about me, all about what *I* needed. That was something that I hadn't ever been able to prioritize before.

I had been a fan of Eric Thomas for a while from his motivational videos. He's got a spark, a way of quickly and clearly getting his point across. You know who he is the minute you hear him speak and I admired that about him.

One of the first real conversations I ever had with Anne was about Eric Thomas, in fact. It was several years ago when I was playing motivational speaker videos on YouTube (for much longer than I should have been, on a date) and asking her, "Do you think I could do this?"

It was the seedling of the ideas that would come to me much more firmly once I started reading.

You Owe You came to me right when I decided to move to California. I got off that phone call with my friend, made up my mind, and walked right into the kitchen to tell Anne about my new plan. Not Florida anymore. California.

Rightfully, she was worried.

I mean, the decision came totally out of the blue. And I'd had a completely different plan the day before. And she and I hadn't been together that long.

"How?" she asked me. "How are you going to do this? You don't even know how to fill out a job application. You can barely read."

I knew, even then, that wasn't the only thing that was worrying her. She knew I wasn't just telling her that I was moving to California.

She knew I was asking her to come with me.

In my hometown city of Bethlehem, I had created a network of people who helped me. I hadn't meant to, but that was the effect of growing up where I did, how I did, and not going anywhere. When I got my license, registered a car, or did my taxes, I had people around who played a part in getting everything done for me. I could never have survived otherwise. It was a large web made of many people who never even knew that I couldn't read. Or maybe they did, but we didn't talk about it.

Anne was a big part of that web. When I made the decision to move, we both realized how much I would have to do on my own and how handicapped I would be when it came to doing it.

For the first time, it became very clear to me that I wasn't, as I used to think, afraid of moving. I was afraid of *reading*. Everything came back to that. Reading was the problem, not moving itself. And, if I wanted to change everything about my life and move to California, I needed to let reading be my map.

So, we had a discussion. Or several discussions. Some arguments, some ups and downs, some ins and outs. My decision to move to California was a major, unintentional test of our relationship. But I knew that I wanted to be with her, and that I was supposed to do *something*. There was a master plan developing in my mind, somewhere. I couldn't see the whole thing, yet, but I knew that this move was part of that master plan.

It was a decision that required me to take 100 percent accountability. I would be totally responsible for my successes and my failures. Eric Thomas's work is deeply tied to my own personal story and gives some context to my discipline. It also sets the sky as the limit and makes it undeniably clear that *you* are the only thing you can actually change.

It doesn't make it *easy*, you know, but that mindset does make it less daunting to tackle major life changes like these.

Anne decided she would come with me. Not to move yet, maybe, but to go check it out.

So, we hopped in the van and drove across the country.

I remember how scared I was during that time. Honestly, I was terrified. The fear was so overwhelming that I could hardly focus on anything else. When we first began driving, I was shaking. My hands were trembling so badly, I could barely grip the steering wheel. I even had to pull over at one point because my foot didn't feel like it was pressing on the gas pedal right. It was like my whole body was betraying me, and I couldn't stop worrying about every little thing that might go wrong. I was a mess of intrusive, irrational fears, the kind of thoughts that kept looping around in my head and wouldn't let go.

Looking back now, it's crazy to think about how much I was fighting against my own mind. But, in hindsight, I can see that it was exactly what I needed. That fear, those doubts—it was all part of the process. I had to go through it. I had to push through the discomfort, to make myself deal with the unknown, to get used to being in a state of change. I had to learn how to cope with shifts, and uncertainty. The only way out was through.

It's clear that I was a fish out of water, evolving to survive in a new environment. I'd never been out of the water so long, but I was starting to gasp in the clean oxygen and if I could hold on through the hard part, I had a feeling I'd see a whole new world.

We didn't stop anywhere along the drive west: no hotels, no planned breaks. We just kept moving. We'd sleep in the van for a few hours, then get up and keep going. The whole thing was a blur—a rapid, unrelenting series of hours on the road. Total highway hypnosis. We slept in shifts when we could, did whatever we had to do to keep the momentum going. In the end, the whole drive only took a little more than two days, but it felt like a lifetime in some ways. Another experience where time bent and changed.

One of the most vivid memories from that trip is when we drove into Los Angeles. I'll never forget seeing all the unhoused people. It was something I wasn't prepared for, especially coming from Pennsylvania. There, homelessness doesn't look like this—it doesn't feel as visible or as widespread. In LA, it was everywhere you looked. You saw it on every street, in every part of town. People struggling, so many people living on the streets, each with their own story. It was a stark reminder of how different life could be, depending on where you are, and how much people in these situations are left to navigate on their own. It was one of those moments that made me think deeply about things I'd never considered before.

I saw all these people holding their signs, and I thought:

Damn.

How the hell am *I* going to make it?

How could I, after everything I'd been through, succeed where these people hadn't? They wrote signs asking for help, saying what their hardship was. They could probably read. I couldn't even *write* a sign!

With no clear direction, we decided to be spontaneous. We'd look up the prettiest beach in Southern California and go wherever Google told us to. No plans, no expectations. Follow the recommendation and see what happens. So, we Googled it, and Google suggested we head to Corona Del Mar. That's where we went.

And let me tell you, Google was spot-on. Corona Del Mar is an absolutely stunning beach. It's one of those places where the moment you see it, you know you've found something special. So, we drove straight there, and for a week, we soaked in the sun and the ocean, enjoying the beauty of it all. It was only me, my workout equipment, my van, my girl, and, well, my dream.

But then, after a week, Anne had to head back to Pennsylvania, so she boarded a plane and left me alone in California.

And there I was, standing on this gorgeous beach, the kind of place you dream about. I was alone. But this time, I had chosen it.

It was both surreal and freeing at the same time. I was exactly where I wanted to be, but simultaneously, I was facing the reality of it. There was something about being by myself in that moment—me and the vastness of the ocean—that made me reflect on everything around me.

From that moment on, every morning when I woke up, my thoughts would go to the people I'd seen on my way in. The people who were living on the side of the road, or those who were huddled under bridges, trying to survive. They stuck with me. The contrast between the beauty of the beach and the harsh reality of the world

I'd driven through upon arrival was something I couldn't ignore. It stayed with me as I went about my days, working on my dream. The disparity between those two worlds—my dream and their struggle—was hard to reconcile, but it was impossible to forget.

Before Anne left, I'd gotten her to write my information on a whiteboard:

Personal Trainer.

100% dedicated.

If you're looking for someone who can bring the gym to you, call me.

I kept her exact writing because I couldn't write anything of my own yet. And her handwriting was nice. If the whiteboard smudged, I had to trace what she had written to make it clear again. My reading was improving, but slowly. Writing was a different (related, but different) skill that didn't come right along with it.

So, I kept that whiteboard in my van, and every day I went down to Corona Del Mar at four in the morning. Every single day for six months straight. And I'd put that sign right there in the sand, or on my van. And I asked people if they were looking for a personal trainer.

The friend I ended up staying with was great. He was an energetic guy, very outgoing. In those early days, he was unbelievably helpful. He lived with his wife, who he'd recently married. They even had a dog together too. It was a vibrant place to land in—a picture-perfect beach, colorful flowers and plants everywhere—and the town was filled with bright buildings and lively restaurants. It seemed like it would be hard to be anything but happy there. In fact, it seemed like everyone there *was* happy.

I don't know if my friend was just offering me help because we came from the same community, or if he was moved by the positivity of the environment. To this day I'm not certain why he reached out to me, or why he offered me so much help. But I'm so glad he did. He told me that California is a place you can live in a van, work out of a van, and exercise on the beach—all that stuff is normal here. He thought I could make way more money doing what I'd been doing in Pennsylvania in California instead. And as soon as I arrived, I could see that he was right.

At this point in my life, I was in the best shape I'd ever been in. I was absolutely ripped—honestly, I couldn't believe how good I looked. I had worked so hard to get there, and now I was seeing the results of all that effort. I understood that efforts could lead to results.

I'd stand there, shirt off, trying to be my own walking advertisement. I mean, why not? I had worked hard for this, and I was proud of it. I'd hang out like that, soaking up the sun, staying out there until ten at night, doing my thing. And slowly, it started happening—people were noticing.

It wasn't long before people were coming up to me and giving me their numbers or just begin chatting. I ended up getting a lot of clients this way. It was crazy. What began as trying to build my presence turned into something more real—like, actual opportunities. I was able to grow my clientele.

At the same time, I was putting a lot of energy into my social media. Back then, it was all about fitness content for me. I'd post videos, workouts, anything that could help showcase my progress and build my brand. My social media wasn't as sophisticated as it is now, but I was still getting a fair amount of engagement by then, and I could see it was helping me connect with people who were into the same things. It felt like everything was clicking at once—building my local clientele and growing my online presence. It was all coming together in a way I hadn't expected.

But I was a trainer! In California! I was in California, and it was working. After some months, I ended up getting a job offer from a gym owner. He walked past me one day, took a card, and gave me a call.

He sat me down shortly after that and told me he wanted to help me. He said he believed in me. "Tell you what," he said. "I'll even pay your first month's rent. No strings attached."

I was still naive, so I thought he was a good guy at first. I didn't have enough experience to think, ah, maybe don't trust him, he's got an ulterior motive. After all, I'd been given a van because of someone's kindness. Been invited to California because of someone's kindness. Maybe I should start believing in the goodness of people.

But over time, his true colors began to show. I began working with him, and it turned out he wanted me to be a piece of eye candy to help him build up his gym. His offer of help *had* come with strings. He didn't want me working on my own stuff, he wanted me to abandon my mission and be his, like, assistant or something.

See, I thought he wanted to help me do what he was doing. I thought he understood that I was passionate about paving my own way, becoming an entrepreneur. But he didn't look at me like that.

Regardless, it was a sort of start. And I worked for him, and then also for other gyms, clients, and so on. I did that for a long time. Until one day, I got home feeling . . . tired.

At the time, I was operating on a deep, strong, and genuine sense of faith. In myself, in things working out. It was something that kept me grounded and gave me the strength to push through tough times. But even with that foundation, I was spiraling into a pretty dark place. I can't say that I completely lost my faith, but I was falling into a deep depression. I was doing my best to fight through it, to keep moving, even though everything felt like it was weighing me down.

The honeymoon was ending. And some new reality was setting in, but I didn't know what it was.

I'll be honest, I was—am—hardheaded. Like, stubborn to a fault. Nobody could tell me anything. I didn't want to hear it. If someone tried to challenge me or push me to do something I wasn't ready for—or if they even just got in my way—I didn't have time for it. I'd shut them out. It was like I had this wall up, and I didn't care who was on the other side of it. I was in this extreme headspace where I was willing to cut anyone off if I felt like they were making things harder for me, even if they had good intentions.

I cut people off in the most drastic ways. I even cut my mom out. I straight-up deleted her number and blocked her. It wasn't even a conversation—it was like I cut out that part of my life completely. The shutdown method, back again as I tried desperately to learn.

And I didn't only do it with her; I was doing the same thing with everyone. If anyone pushed me, or if I didn't vibe with what they were saying or doing, I would cut ties. I didn't want anyone's influence messing with the bubble I'd created around myself. I barely had a safe space yet, not like back home where I'd built it over decades. Anne had already gone home; she'd only come out to get me here and take a trip. She couldn't move right away.

In California, I was exposed. Completely alone. I was living in this place where I felt like I had to protect myself from everyone and everything—even the people who loved me most.

But it was necessary. Before I did that, there were so many people in my ear telling me to do *this*, plan for *that*, whatever. I was trying to hear my own voice for the first time in my life. I needed silence.

I was wild. People would see videos of me running up and down Newport Beach, filmed by me or other people, and I would be screaming, "Yo, I'm going to be the best trainer!" I was running on the street screaming, and people thought I was crazy—can't imagine why!

But man, I was crazy. People would call me and ask why I was running around screaming in the street and I wouldn't even answer them. I'd block them and delete their number. And those were friends, cousins, people I'd known my whole life. It felt like: you question me, you get cut off. I felt like I needed to be that way because I couldn't explain what I was doing to them. I just had to do it. Nobody would understand. I needed to be on my own. I think it's like when most people leave home for the first time as teenagers, go off to college or whatever, they start fighting with their family. Time to leave the nest kinda thing.

Of those people, the only one I've reconnected with since is my mom. I've exchanged a happy birthday or two with some of the other people. I didn't cut them off because they had done something wrong, I felt like I needed to isolate myself. It was impossible to explain the way I was feeling to everyone, so I didn't. *You Owe You.* I owed me. I pushed myself out of the nest and I didn't want anyone's help.

But after I'd been at this a while, I wanted something more.

I wanted people to know more about me. The truth about me. I didn't want to be a fitness trainer my whole life.

By the time I realized this, I had gotten my first apartment in California. Anne had come out to live with me. We settled in, made our little home and kitchen, our nest. And things were working.

But I knew I had more in me. I wanted to *be* more.

"If you've got more in you," Anne challenged me, "you should tell TikTok more about you. Why are you just giving them fitness? Why don't you tell them you've got OCD, tell them you can't read?"

Yup, it was Anne's idea. One I'll be forever thankful for.

Not that I agreed right away.

"Oh, hell no," I said, not even wanting to entertain the idea. "Nobody wants to hear that!"

Yeah, that's what I thought. Maybe because of all the times I got smacked as a kid and heard, "Boy, no one wants to hear about that!" when I talked about my feelings.

"You're not the only one," she insisted.

"To me I am."

"You could help other people. People like you who need a little more *motivation* to get going and work on themselves."

That reminded me of my bigger goal. I wanted to be a motivational speaker—which meant I needed to motivate people. Maybe, just maybe, this was my chance to start.

That October, when I'd been in California for about a year, I went out to my van to record the video that would change my life forever. This is where we began, right? I was scared. I wasn't sure it was a good idea. There were a million reasons *not* to do it.

Didn't matter. I sat down, set up the camera, and spoke. You know the words now, say them with me:

"What's up? I can't read."

9

READING IS COMMUNITY

The Diary of a Young Girl (1947), by Anne Frank
The Outsiders (1967), by S. E. Hinton

I've got to admit, things took off in a way I never expected. Yeah, I knew I was telling my truth to a lot of people, but I figured I'd get a few comments at most, and everyone would maybe think a little less of me or wish me luck—but either way I figured they'd forget about it in ten minutes and that would be that.

That's not how it went. People took notice. Thousands of people commented, some congratulating me on telling my truth, some saying they were once in a similar position, others telling me the system was set up to let me and my brothers and sisters fail. I didn't want to get into the politics of it all, but it was nice to know there were people out there who weren't . . . I don't know, mean about it? What had I expected from people?

BookTok showed up to cheer me on and help me out. People I'd never heard of and who hadn't heard of me before that one video took off came on to suggest their favorite books. It seemed like my declaration reminded those who already could read that it was a gift they should be enjoying more. It showed others like me who can't read that they're not alone.

Looking back, I don't think it was only Anne's encouragement that led me there—though I credit her with it. But I had to be in a place to hear her. And I think I was just tired. Tired of being confused. Tired of lagging behind everyone else. Tired of hiding it. Tired of not living up to a potential I *knew* that I had inside. I was sick to death of compromising who I was as a person, just to survive. I wasn't as likable as I wanted to be; people saw me as defensive and argumentative, and I was. I wasn't as flexible as I wanted to be, either—I had to feel comfortable, and in a known situation.

When I started getting bigger on TikTok, one of the very first things I did was ask for book recommendations. I knew that if I wanted to change my life, I needed to begin somewhere, and I figured there was no better way than by learning from the people who had been reading their whole lives. So, in October 2022, I asked my followers what I should start with. A lot of the books I've shared with you so far were ones I was told to pick up by my followers.

I wasn't expecting such an overwhelming response, but right away, two titles stood out: *The Outsiders* by S. E. Hinton and *The Diary of a Young Girl* by Anne Frank.

I remember looking at those titles and thinking about what it meant that those were the first books people thought I should read. One was a classic coming-of-age story about kids trying to survive in a world that didn't make things easy for them. The other was a deeply personal diary of a girl navigating life in hiding during one of history's darkest times. Two completely different books, but both about resilience. Both about finding meaning in impossible circumstances.

So, one day I decided to act. I went straight to the library, got myself a card, and checked out both books.

That moment was bigger than it might seem. It wasn't only about getting books—it was about stepping into a place I had always felt like I didn't belong. Libraries had never been my space. They had always been these quiet, foreign places, filled with people who seemed to know exactly what they were doing—people flipping through pages; studying; sucked in by words that, for most of my life, had felt completely out of reach for me. I used to walk past libraries without a second thought, assuming they weren't meant for someone like me.

But now, I was stepping into that world on purpose, for me. I wasn't just someone who couldn't read—I was someone *learning* to read. That shift in identity was powerful. It made me feel like I was claiming something that had always been waiting for me, something I had been kept away from for too long. And holding those books in my hands, knowing I had chosen them, knowing I was about to read them—it felt like opening a door I had spent my whole life standing outside of.

At the time, I had this great synergy going between working out and reading. It was like mental and physical health were all part of the same workout, you know? So, I'd read while I worked out, and let me tell you, it was exhilarating. Exhilarating and intense.

And those were some intense books to start with.

Especially *The Diary of a Young Girl* by Anne Frank. That book hit me hard. It was the first thing I could actually read, and it made me think about my life in ways I hadn't before. I'd never heard of Anne Frank or her famous diary before I read it. I didn't know very much about her, the Holocaust, or World War II. It opened my eyes to all the things, all the lived experiences in the world that I couldn't understand—even if I *could* read about them—and how people's experiences are so completely different. How bad life can be. How beautiful too. It gave me a lot to reflect on.

All of it had me looking at my own life and thinking, *I'm just a human living on the planet in the twenty-first century, trying to be happy, and I feel lucky to be here.*

This was a time of a lot of change. I mean *a lot.* My partner, Anne, had just found out she was pregnant. So much was happening all at once. But for once, I wasn't being pushed around by it all. I had chosen my life now. I was with Anne because I loved her. I was reading and beginning to get it. I had a new community online. The unexpected news of a baby on the way? It didn't send me spiraling like it might have at another time in my life.

I was excited. But I was also in a life I didn't recognize. Even though it was good—way better than it had ever been, in fact—it made me feel a little like I was in a dream.

I loved the response I got from people on my videos, and I love my community now, but something about the way everything came together back then . . . I guess it stressed me out. I fixated on the (relatively few) negative comments I received. There were some people mocking me, others laughing at me, and even some racists. They didn't represent most of the people who interacted with me, but it was some of them. And it was, I guess, what I'd always been afraid of.

I was also realizing, once things were being put into perspective, that I didn't actually like fitness instructing. Not specifically, anyway. No, the part I liked about it was making people feel good, making people feel *motivated.* What I'd hoped for all along.

It was so much change at once, and even though most of it was good, it was all getting to me.

Being in California and not wanting to drink alcohol (I'll talk about my sobriety later on), it seemed there was only one thing that could help me try to cope with everything that was happening: weed. So, I started smoking weed. A *lot* of weed. Definitely too much for a while there, and ultimately, I'd cut it off the same way I ended up doing with booze—pretty much cold turkey. But I was barely getting by, at that point. Coping. Not thriving.

Don't get me wrong. A lot of what was going on felt *amazing*. It was kind of like the excitement you feel on your first day of school. Like, yeah, maybe you might be stressed that summer's ending, but you're also excited to put on a new outfit, meet new people, see people you haven't seen since last school year. It felt like a purpose, like I finally had a career, and not just a job. It still feels like that.

I've always wanted to be someone who changed the world. Ever since I was a kid, I had this feeling deep in my gut that I was supposed to *matter* somehow, that I wasn't just meant to drift through life unnoticed. But for the longest time, I had no idea how I was supposed to do that. I didn't think I had the tools. I didn't think I was capable. But when I started to learn how to read, when I began making real progress, something in me shifted.

For the first time, it felt like changing the world wasn't some distant dream—it was in fact within my reach. I could help other people who couldn't read, I could make a real difference in their lives; I could help kids like me before they had to struggle the way I did. Maybe I could even write a book one day. Maybe I could use my own life, my own struggles, to help someone else find their way.

All these thoughts were bouncing around in my head, and more. Suddenly, the world wasn't only what was right in front of me—it was *open*. The possibilities stretched out in every direction. Things I'd never even considered now felt like they were within my reach. Maybe I could own a house. Maybe I could have real money in my bank account, not small cash to scrape by, but enough to truly feel secure. Maybe I could buy my mama a house.

That was the unexpected power of reading. It opened my mind to possibilities, gave me the incentive to try new things. It made me feel like there were road maps to all kinds of success and I could choose from any number of routes.

And that was what I'd been missing.

You gotta understand—before this, I genuinely could not conceive of things that, for some people, might have been common sense. I never understood how a person—a regular-ass human, the same kind of being that I am—could grow up and become a lawyer, or a doctor, or build rockets and shit. I thought those people were born different. Like, some people just came into the world already knowing things, already meant for success. They were given the gift of that knowledge.

And me? I wasn't.

It was like being a peasant in medieval times. Some people are kings. Some are farmers. And if you're a farmer, that's just what you are. That's all you'll ever be. There's no way to cross that line. No way to change your fate.

But now, for the first time in my life, I could see how I could become a king.

Or a doctor. Or a lawyer. Or a writer. Or a TikToker.

Before, I knew other people had done it. I knew people went viral, knew they were out there making money on TikTok or YouTube, doing it as a job. But I didn't know how. It felt like another one of those mysteries, another one of those things that other people got to do, not me. But now, I was realizing—that could be me too.

I wasn't even all that great at being a fitness instructor, to be honest. I mean, I was good at motivating people, and the physical stuff came naturally to me. But the people who were making real money at it weren't simply coaching—they were building something. They were making programs, selling twelve-week courses, branding themselves. And I couldn't do that. Not back then. Not when I could barely read or write. I wasn't running a business—I was freelancing. Living off tips. Barely getting by.

But on TikTok?

On TikTok, I didn't have to be anybody that I wasn't. I didn't have to pretend to be a businessman or an expert. I didn't have to write complicated shit or fake like I had it all figured out.

All I had to be was *me*.

The guy who was learning to read.

And people cared.

And it wasn't only random people scrolling by, people looking for entertainment—it was educators too. Actual teachers. The exact kind of help I had needed my whole damn life. The kind of one-on-one attention I should've gotten twenty years ago but never did. And now?

Now I had thousands of educators willing to help me.

It was the craziest thing. The few times in my childhood when a teacher sat down with me and gave me the time I needed, I did really well. That was when I learned best. But that kind of attention was rare. I didn't get it enough to grow.

Until now.

Now, if I hopped on TikTok Live right this second, I'd get hundreds of educators who would sit there and teach me. Because they wanted to. Because they cared.

It's such a gift.

I mean, the people in my community aren't merely spectators. They don't simply watch from the sidelines. They show up. They log on. They talk to me. They encourage me. They tell me what I'm doing right, and also where I can improve.

I always have somebody there who cares about me and my life.

That's wild.

If I'm reading on stream, other people will hop on and read the same book with me. It's about more than learning—it's about connection. This is the kind of community I needed when I was a kid. Not just people to teach me, but people who were *there*. People who wanted to grow with me. People who could sit in comfortable silence and *exist* together, the way I never got to.

Growing up, I couldn't just sit down with some friends and read a book.

Man, I wish I could have.

But now? Now I have that. And I don't know what I did to deserve it, but I'm holding onto it for dear life.

Maybe they see something in me that I don't even see in myself.

Maybe I'm helping them the way they're helping me.

Or maybe they're proof that the world still has good people in it. The kind of people you don't always believe exist. People who are *kind*, just because.

Angels, straight up.

It's funny to say this, since I didn't get that kind of support from people in my real life, but no matter what I go through now, I know my angels are there. And I've never had that before—not outside of my partner.

But these people.

They lift me up.

They keep me connected to the world when I feel like I'm drifting. When I'm too deep in my own head.

Those people are everything to me.

I think everybody needs that. I know Anne will be there for me no matter what, the way I would for her. And I think that's kind of like reading. Like, you can't really live—you can't take risks, you can't try to build a better life—without a safety net. Without *community*. Without people who've got you, even when you don't got yourself.

When you fall, they help you back up.

A lot of people don't have that.

Like the people I saw on the way into Los Angeles. A lot of them had lost all that connection. And it's not fair. It's not right. Everybody should have a community.

Because that's why we survived as a species. That's why we aren't still out in the wilderness, fighting for scraps. That's why we didn't go extinct.

We had each other.

And you can't build anything without that. Not yourself, not a city, not a government. You can't invent cars, go to the moon, develop AI—nothing. Everything we do, we do together. For better or worse.

And with reading, and especially with TikTok, I started seeing something I'd never seen before: how many communities I was already a part of.

I'm one of the people who has dyslexia. I'm one of the kids who grew up rough. I went to special ed. I'm neurodivergent. I'm an adult who couldn't read.

Those are all communities, and I'm a part of all of them. Always was, even though I didn't know it.

And social media lets all of us find each other.

When I got on TikTok and told the world that I couldn't read, I was telling everyone what group I was a part of. And suddenly, the people in that group could find me.

And that's part of what this book is about too.

By telling the world who I am, where I come from, and what I've been through, I'm reaching out to the people who see themselves in my story.

And maybe that's how I figure out the role I was always meant to play.

And *that* is where this chapter's other inspirational book, *The Outsiders*, comes in.

The Outsiders isn't just a story—it's a mirror. It's about the reality of social divides, the way people get trapped by the labels society puts on them and how those labels can shape your entire life whether you want them to or not. It's about the way people are sorted into groups, not only because of who they are, but because of where they come from, what they look like, how much money their family has, and the assumptions people make about them before they even get a chance to speak. It's about loyalty, loss, and the fight to be seen for more than your circumstances.

I related to the main character, Ponyboy Curtis, a fourteen-year-old orphan in Oklahoma who was in a gang of greasers with his older brothers. Like me, Ponyboy is trying to understand the world beyond what he'd been told. He isn't satisfied with what he's been given—he wants *more*. He has this curiosity, this hunger to see the world from a different perspective, even though he is constantly being pulled back into the same cycle, the same gang fights, the same expectations. It reminded me of the way I grew up, the way I felt stuck in one way of life because that was all I had ever known. But deep down, I knew there had to be more. Ponyboy had that same feeling. He *saw* things differently, but no matter what, the world refused to see *him* differently.

And then there's Ponyboy's best friend, Johnny Cade. Johnny is a good kid. He has a big heart. But the world didn't care about that. The world didn't ask. The world didn't stop to consider what he'd been through, what kind of person he was inside. It only saw the things he'd done in a moment of fear and desperation. And once the world decided what he was, there was no changing it.

That hit me so hard.

I've seen so many people like Johnny—kids who never had a fair shot, kids who got thrown into bad situations and never got the chance to get out. And I almost became one myself. It's so easy for one mistake, one moment, to define you forever. People love to judge from the outside, love to make assumptions about who you are based on things that are out of your control. Where you were born. What kind of family you come from. Whether or not you had a dad in your life. Whether or not you had money. And if you slip up, even once, even for a second, they're ready to write you off completely.

But then there's *staying gold*—from the famous scene in *The Outsiders* where Johnny tells Ponyboy to "stay gold." The idea that there's something pure in all of us, something worth holding onto, no matter how rough the world gets. That's what made me *feel* that book deep in my chest. It's about innocence, but not in a childish way. It's about holding onto the part of yourself that still believes in something. That still hopes. That still sees beauty, even when life is ugly. That still—at least—tries to be good, even when the world isn't fair.

Reading gave me that.

Reading gave me a way to hold onto hope. A way to understand that even though the world wants to put people into boxes, I don't have to stay in one. It showed me that I wasn't alone in how I felt—that there were other people, even fictional ones, who had gone through the same thing, felt the same frustration, the same need to be more than what the world expected. Reading gave me a way to *stay gold* even when everything in life was trying to make me hard.

The truth is, life throws a lot at you. It's easy to let the world make you bitter, to let experience wear you down. It's easy to build walls, to stop trusting, to stop caring. It's easy to let anger be your fuel because anger can make you feel powerful. But reading, learning, *growing*—those things keep you soft in the right ways. They keep you *human*. They keep you open to understanding people, and yourself.

And I think that's what *The Outsiders* is basically about. It's about fighting for your identity, refusing to be just one thing, refusing to let the world tell you who you are. It's about knowing that no matter what's happened to you, you still have a choice in the kind of person you want to be. It's about holding onto something good inside yourself, even when life tries to take it away.

For me, reading gave me that same power.

The power to define myself. And after a lifetime of it, I was starting to see myself as part of something bigger. Not just as an outsider.

10

READING IS A DRUG

The Alchemist (1993), by Paulo Coelho

Reading is a drug. It's mind-altering, escapist, and fun. It stimulates the brain, therapeutically, and hits you with emotional highs and lows. It can fuck you up, it can heal you, it can excite you and, yes, it can bore you. It can save your life. It can give you so many new ideas that you can't stop talking to your friends about everything you learned, how it stretched your imagination.

As I read books that were recommended to me, I honestly felt like I was tripping. I was suddenly somersaulting through time and space into worlds and minds different from my own. And how was it that there was this crazy magic that no matter how different my life was from the characters' lives in the books I read, I could see myself in their stories?

The more I learned, the less I knew. But the more I seemed to understand.

We all live our lives under the assumption that we're controlling something. You think that you can do something in five minutes—that's you trying to control your experience of time. But when I was in a car accident at nineteen, time slowed down like Neo dodging bullets in *The Matrix*.

During the crash, being thrown around the car, nothing else mattered. I couldn't think of anything besides *am I going to die?* But when the car stopped moving, life came back. That's how something time-altering hits you. Suddenly you can feel again, breathe again. You feel the temperature outside, it's all there again. The pain oozes in.

I remember waking up in a field after the crash and thinking, *What the hell?* Like, *I'm okay . . . but what was that? What's going on now?* Just complete confusion and disorientation.

Because of the intensity of that experience, I've never been able to completely let it go. The feeling never goes away. To this day, I can sit here and relive it in crystal clear detail. There was something so surreal about it that I didn't understand. How years fit into minutes, and how that way of thinking never left.

Now, for me, reading is very similar. Imagine never having . . . imagined. Never having heard someone tell a story before. Only ever hearing about real events your whole life, but then suddenly jumping into fantasy and needing to cope with the difference between reality and imagination. My "imagination muscle" was atrophied.

There's a group of indigenous people I learned about called the Pirahã; a linguist who lived among them reported that their language doesn't include the past or future tense, and that they live completely in the present. In a way, I can relate to this. I grew up without learning or discovering anything but the here and now, and I wasn't using my imagination at all. I not only had no history or frame of reference, but I was shaped by their absence. Not only was I missing them, but I was also missing the space for them.

Readers may take understanding and comprehension for granted, but what they are doing is diving into worlds through words, feeling emotions that aren't their own, seeing landscapes through descriptions that might have next to nothing in common with their lived experiences. It's powerful, spiritual, and soul deep. A whole life of experience can fit into a biography that takes two hours to read. And while you're in a cozy chair all afternoon with a good book, it can feel like no time has passed at all.

I had a limited life up until I started to read and share my experience online. It caused a massive wave of new ideas and ways of living to crash over me. I couldn't go back. Like the near-death experience I had during the car accident, embarking on this journey forever transformed my perspective.

It's dangerous for a person to get a shock to the brain like that. It would be like if your body grew up superfast all at once. You'd get killer growing pains. You'd feel stretched, bizarre in the space you occupied. I went to the emergency room three times overall. I was literally losing myself as I changed. I am still losing myself, but now I'm more comfortable with the fact that losing yourself is how you find yourself.

Gaining this ability to look inward opens up your brain in ways you can't even imagine. It's so cool. It makes me think of being a kid. Growing up, you want so badly to be an adult, a superhero, rich, good-looking, something greater than yourself at that time. Whatever it is that calls to you, whatever you can imagine becoming.

This process has taken me back to that childlike state of dreaming and growing. I have to ask myself all the questions that feel normal when you know nothing, when you know you're meant to be growing. But here I am trying to become who I want to be when I grow up, having already grown up.

It's a gift and a curse to understand that you can have something and achieve something greater than yourself. It's so comfortable and so unsettling at the same time. The world is your oyster, but damn . . . that's a big oyster. And you've got to shuck it yourself.

When I talk about this experience, a lot of people tell me it sounds trippy and philosophical, and they're not wrong. Alcohol, weed, and other drugs can relax you, lower your inhibitions, and push you through the motions of this kind of feeling, but then the high wears off. And coming down usually leaves you feeling way worse than before, in my experience.

Actually *doing* the work to turn inward has a lasting effect on the way your consciousness functions. This is something I want to share with younger people who find themselves in the same trap I was in, because it's another way to feel good rather than drugs. It expands the mind even more. Imagine a young kid getting addicted to the positive aspects of what learning about the world can do. What they're looking for by getting high can be found in reading. I know some sixteen-year-olds might think it sounds lame, but I wish I could ask them to try.

Instead of relying on alcohol and weed and opioids—in other words, instead of inviting struggle, desensitization, and fear—we could invite hope, growth, and positivity. For me, reading, in particular, cuts deep for several reasons: my family, my school experience, my ADHD and OCD, and even my race and our history.

For people in situations like mine, the ability to go to another space is powerful. It forces you to take on new perspectives, live a new life, and grow beyond yourself in your mind. It rewires you, and brings you back to a young state of mind, ready to grow. I feel like I'm a little high all the time these days. I'm loving the process of getting smarter, feeling better about myself because of it, and having a wider world at my fingertips. I get to keep that with me forever. It'll never go away.

* * *

It's my belief that reading is that launching pad, no matter what your personal struggle is to overcome. It just so happens that my biggest one *is* reading in and of itself. And in learning to read, I am slowly curing the other parts of me.

I want to share the power of reading with the world, but how many people like me will believe it? Those who've grown up in the hood—maybe they're in prison, maybe they can't believe reading can do anything for them. If only they knew that their biggest struggle could lead to their greatest change, we'd break so many cycles.

I'll ask, "Why do you want money? Why do you want fame? Why are you selling shit? Why are you doing this criminal thing and risking the consequences? Why are you doing *any* of this?"

And then:

"Have you ever thought about reading?"

And they'll respond with something like, "What the hell is reading going to do?"

But what *is* reading? Everything's in there—everything is in reading, without exception. New points of view, worlds, lives, ideas, approaches, everything. Reading gives you the opportunity to be anything long enough to believe it. Then it gives you the tools to make it happen.

Part of the process of evolving is exercising knowledge. Not only knowing that things can be different somehow, but knowing how they might be different, and having the ability to make that *real.* Many who have committed crimes can see the mistakes they've made, but they still don't change. Why? It's like a short circuit in a lightbulb. They have the motivation, the electricity, to make the change, but no pathway to get it to the light. So what happens? The electricity feeds right back into the power source and eventually the circuit—the person—repeats the cycle until it burns out. These individuals are not operating with everything they need to succeed. They need new ideas. They need new bulbs.

I have talked to people like that, people like I knew growing up, people like I was. Through the sharing of ideas, some see a path forward. You'll see empathy, emotion, even tears and anger. All kinds of feelings happen when they're given even the slightest relief from their lives.

Every day you read you build more empathy, more vocabulary, and more courage. It happens over time.

As you read, you start to learn. Even if you don't mean to. It's weird, but it feels like unlocking. Like when you play a video game and unlock another level. It's like, *Oh, I've downloaded* empathy, *I can light up that bulb when I need to. Now I need to learn when and how to use it.*

Now, it's not all sunshine after that point. Once you ask yourself, *So how do I use it?* you see that it's a shit ton of work. And it's only one of the words that you need to be able to learn and incorporate to be a part of society. It's an uphill battle.

But then after some time, either you meet someone, or you see a character in a book, and you find your words in there. You'll see a character who's a monk, and they'll hold a mirror up to you. Who could have imagined that? You're over the moon because you realize that you have twenty new words that are core parts of you, and you know how to maneuver those words. When anger pops up for that character and they're like, "Yeah, I know anger, but I am not my anger," it can be a validating experience, and can even inform the ways you'll want to grow next. Maybe the character expresses fears that you've felt alone with before, and once you read their story, you can say, *Okay, this is a human thing I'm feeling, and it's allowed. I don't need to fight it.*

I used this new ability to home in on the happiness at my core. I never let it go. I experience my other feelings fully, but knowing, and importantly *choosing* who I am—that gives me the power to be happy in a room full of angry people.

And yet there's nothing wrong with crying, fear, or negative emotions. There are no bad emotions. They're human. You are human. The thing that makes that dude steal some shit to get drugs? Those same feelings exist in a toddler, in your grandmother, in me. Reading shows you different choices. Different ways to use the feelings we all have.

When I read *The Alchemist*, I saw myself in the main character, Santiago the shepherd, immediately. Not because I was out herding sheep. But because he had a dream, and he had to fight everything to believe it was possible. The whole world around him was set up to tell him no. To tell him, *You're a lowly shepherd, stay in your place.* But he knew there was something more. Even when he didn't know exactly what that *more* was, he could feel it. That's what lit a fire under me when I picked up that book for the first time.

Reading it felt like unlocking a hidden part of my brain. It was one of the first books that made me feel like reading wasn't just some pastime, some skill I was supposed to pick up to get by. This was the key to something bigger. That shepherd wasn't simply reading words—he was reading the world. He was reading signs, people, moments. He was learning how to listen, not only with his ears but with his mind. And that's what reading was doing for me. It wasn't merely giving me words; it was giving me *vision*.

There's a part in the book where Santiago starts to understand the "Language of the World," where he realizes that everything—every obstacle, every person he meets, every delay—is part of the odyssey. That's how I felt about learning to read. At first, it was humiliating.

I'd stumble over words, I'd get frustrated, I'd hear people in my own head telling me it didn't matter. But every time I picked up a book and kept going, it felt like I was tapping into something bigger than myself.

And here's the crazy part—the more I read, the more I began to believe in my own dreams. That's what the shepherd in the book learned too. He didn't wait for someone else to tell him his dream was real. He *knew* it was, and because he kept chasing it, the whole universe began to shift to make it possible. That's the realest thing I've ever read.

When you don't know how to read, your world is small. You might not realize it. You might even think it's comfortable the way it is. Until you run into the walls, which becomes more and more frequent. Because when your world is small, your opportunities are small. Your dreams are small—not because you don't have the capacity to dream big, but because you don't have the tools to stretch beyond what's in front of you. But once you start reading—really *reading*—you see what's possible. You see proof that people like you have made it out, have made something of themselves, have fought and won. You see the steps, the pathways, the patterns.

Santiago the shepherd boy had to trust the process. He had to leave behind what was comfortable and step into the unknown. That's what I had to do too. Learning to read as an adult wasn't easy, but every new word I learned was another step toward something bigger. Just as Santiago followed the signs, I followed the books. And the books led me here and into the unknown.

That's what it felt like to start reading. An unfamiliar landscape. Like Santiago in *The Alchemist*, I learned that all the doubt and stress along the way was part of the bigger picture.

In the book, Santiago meets an Englishman who is obsessed with books but who doesn't understand the deeper meaning of the world. Meanwhile, Santiago trusts in the Soul of the World, the alchemical principle of interconnection. That was me too. At first, I thought reading was only about decoding words, getting through pages, proving I could do it, getting to a finish line. But the more I read, the more I felt what Santiago felt. That everything is connected.

Which is the same kind of shit your friend says when he's stoned in the basement.

But for real. Santiago had to leave behind part of his flock; I left behind parts of myself. The parts that told me it was too late, or that I wasn't smart enough.

When I say reading is a drug, I mean it in a good way, even though I don't have drugs in my life anymore (besides reading). Reading changes your mind and opens you up to new perspectives. It makes you ask questions like, *What if the sky isn't blue?*

Trippy, right?

11

READING IS SOBERING

The Moth Presents: A Point of Beauty: True Stories of Holding On and Letting Go (2024), edited by The Moth

Speaking of drugs.

My sobriety.

Beginning to understand why I did the things I did also helped me understand why other people did what they did. It's one thing to reflect on your own life, to analyze your choices and figure out the reasons behind them, but when you take that same mindset and apply it to other people, everything shifts. You stop seeing actions as random or irrational, and you learn to recognize the underlying emotions, patterns, unspoken fears, and motivations that shape the way people behave.

This is especially true in relationships. When people get into fights, not having that kind of empathy can be a huge problem. So many arguments happen because one or both people can't step outside of their own perspective long enough to see where the other person is coming from. You gotta be able to recognize why someone you love might be mad at you without jumping to the conclusion that they hate you. That sounds obvious, but when you're in the middle of it—when emotions are running high, when you feel attacked or misunderstood—it isn't always that clear. It's easy to react instead of reflect.

And even when a relationship ends, that same kind of understanding still matters. Just because two people go through a breakup doesn't mean they experience it the same way. Their individuality means they didn't even experience the relationship the same way. One person might feel relief while the other feels devastation. One might need space while the other wants closure. It's not a shared experience so much as two separate ones happening at the same time, and I think that's something a lot of people don't realize until they've been through it themselves.

Lately, I've been doing a lot of learning, a lot of growth. I'm in a place where I value speaking calmly, trying to listen, trying to have real discussions instead of just reacting. As a parent, that's extra important . . . and it gives me a *lot* of opportunity to practice. So that's the kind of thing I'm working on. But I've also had to accept that not everybody is in that same place. Not everyone is on the same journey of self-discovery that I'm on. And because I've changed doesn't mean everyone else has to.

That's been hard for me. Learning isn't a straight line—it's this constant back-and-forth where every new realization distorts what you thought you already understood. You think you've got a handle on something, you think you finally get it, and then suddenly, you see it from a whole new angle, and it's almost the opposite of what you thought before. It's humbling. It makes you realize how much of your worldview is shaped by your habits, your environment, and the little unspoken rules you've been following your whole life without even questioning them.

If all you've ever done in a fight is yell, then yelling is the only tool you've got. If no one ever taught you how to pause, how to breathe, how to *listen* before responding, then how are you supposed to magically know how to do it? The world doesn't work like that. People act according to what they know. They react the way they've always reacted until something forces them to change.

A lot of my growth has been about breaking those patterns. Rewiring the way I deal with conflict, the way I handle stress, the way I treat myself when things get hard. And that includes—and especially—drinking and drugs.

Growing up, I didn't do illicit drugs. Not much, anyway. I was around them, but they weren't something I leaned into, at least not at the start. I remember one of the first times I tried smoking weed. I didn't know much about it—I was just a kid, going along with the crowd, taking a few hits because that's what everyone else was doing. Because *why not?*

It's only weed, right? Everybody talked about it. And people *love* it. It's in songs, in movies, on TV. It seemed harmless to me.

One day when I was about fourteen, I was at my friend's house, thinking I was gonna get a little high and chill like everybody else. But I got way too high. I thought I'd only taken a few hits, but suddenly, I was on another planet. I wasn't just dizzy or giggly—I was losing time, losing control. My body felt like it wasn't mine. A thousand hands were on me at once, voices surrounding me, saying my name, asking if I was okay. It was terrifying.

I sat there staring at everyone, trying to figure out if it was real or if I was dreaming. And the thing is, this wasn't like modern dispensary weed. We were just kids smoking whatever we could get our hands on. Who knows what was in it? It could've been laced, or maybe I was too inexperienced to handle it. Either way, I was in full-blown panic mode.

I was sweating like crazy, and in my dazed, irrational state, I did the most natural thing I could think of:

I stripped off all my clothes and ran out of the house.

Seriously. Just took off, sprinting down the street like some kind of wild animal. My mind was racing, my heart pounding. Then, suddenly, I noticed it was raining. The cold drops hitting my skin shocked me back into reality, at least a little bit. I realized I couldn't go home like this—I was, I remembered, high as shit—so I turned around and ran back to my friend's house, grabbed my clothes, and got dressed again.

But I was still freaking out. I kept telling everyone that something was wrong, that we needed to call the police. Unsurprisingly, nobody was very into that idea.

I didn't care. I went ahead and did it myself. I called the cops on myself. And the funniest part? My friends were so high that they just sat there and watched me make the call.

When the cops showed up, that's when reality hit for everyone else. The second the police knocked on the door, my friends scattered like roaches. I was the only one left. I opened the door, looked right at the officers, and told them, completely seriously, "Something is wrong with me."

They took me to the hospital. I don't remember much after that, only passing out and waking up in my house days later.

That was the last time I touched weed for a long, long while. At the time, I didn't realize how long it would be before I even thought about it again.

Then, in high school, I started drinking, figuring that was safer. It wasn't something that happened overnight. It crept in slowly. It began with me visiting friends who had already moved on to college, and I remember feeling kind of grown-up and cool when they'd pull out a few beers or something stronger. I hadn't drunk much up until then, but when I was around them, it seemed natural to join in. I was eager to be part of their world. After that, I would drink more on my own or with my high school friends. It wasn't anything wild at first.

In the beginning, we'd only drink at parties or casual gatherings. Every weekend, sometimes every other weekend, we'd all chip in to buy forties or a six-pack or whatever, and that would be that. It was the kind of thing that felt like part of being a teenager—experimenting with new experiences and trying to figure out who we were.

Looking back, it wasn't even about getting drunk—it was more about the social experience. We didn't know what we were doing, but that was part of the fun. A couple of drinks was more than enough to get us feeling tipsy, and because none of us had built up a tolerance yet, we never needed to drink more than that. It wasn't about pushing boundaries or testing how far we could go—it was about hanging out, laughing, and being silly with each other. We never had any big plans to party hard or do anything too out-of-control. We were just kids, having fun.

Drinking, for a long time, seemed to bring out the best in us. It didn't cause fights or drama—at least, not for us. Maybe it was because we were all in that same naive phase where everything like this felt new and exciting. Drinking felt like a way to open ourselves up. It made us feel more confident, more carefree. We'd dance our hearts out at house parties, joke around, act a little crazy—but always in the spirit of fun. I think that's pretty common for a lot of young people, at least in the early stages. Drinking wasn't something that weighed us down. It was hard to see it as anything but a part of growing up.

But over the years, things started to change. What had been an occasional thing, something we did for fun on the weekends, began to grow into something more regular. The carefree drinking I used to enjoy was feeling more like a habit, something I needed to keep doing, something that had become a regular part of my life. Before I knew it, I found myself drinking almost every night. It didn't matter what day of the week it was—I'd find a reason to go out and have a few drinks.

There were weeks where I'd go out every single night. I might take Sundays off, but even then, I'd end up having a drink or two to wind down. It wasn't about needing to drink to get through the day, but it was something I did out of routine, something that was always there. It didn't seem dangerous at first. It felt like it was part of who I was—I was the same person I'd always been, only now, I was doing it more often.

Drinking not only became a part of my identity, but it also took a toll on me in ways I didn't fully understand at the time. I wasn't thinking about the long-term effects of alcohol. It turned into a way of life, and I didn't question it.

And then, I ended up in prison. You might expect that would be the end of my drinking. It should have been, but it wasn't. You'd think that being locked up would be the moment where I'd finally be forced to get clean, to sit with myself, to rethink everything. But even in prison, I wasn't completely done with drinking.

It wasn't something I did regularly there—not like before. But I still remember that one Christmas when a couple of my fellow inmates and I managed to get our hands on a bottle. I don't even remember exactly how we got it; those things simply happened in places like that. Word got around, and before long, we were passing it around, each of us taking our share like it was some kind of sacred ritual. And just like that, I was drunk. Like old times.

There was something strange about it—something that felt almost normal, like I had carried a piece of my old life into this completely different world. I was locked up, in a place that was supposed to strip me of all the habits and vices I had on the outside. And yet, here I was, doing the same thing I'd always done. Maybe that should've told me something, but at the time, I wasn't thinking that deeply about it. I was just drinking.

Even after that, once I left prison and was technically "free," I didn't completely let go of drinking.

I guess it was ingrained in me. Society does that to you to some extent—makes alcohol feel like it's just a part of life, something you do without questioning it. But for me, it was deeper than that. I had my parents as examples. And neither of them ever let drinking go either.

I don't think I've ever seen my dad without a drink in his hand. (I'll talk about him soon, by the way.) But no, not once.

And my mom? She was a heavy drinker too, though she has long since stopped by the time I write this book. I grew up watching her drink, living in it. And the thing is, when you grow up in an environment like that, it doesn't feel like anything's wrong. It feels like life. It's what you know.

That was hard to deal with sometimes. There were moments that stuck with me—times when I'd have something important going on at school, and my mom would show up drunk. It made me angry, but at the same time, I felt like I understood why. Life was hard. Harder than I even realized back then. I don't know if that was the reason she drank so much, or if she was wired that way, but it was a constant in her life.

She wasn't the kind of person who went out to bars or got wasted at clubs. Instead, she was one of those people who drank at home. That was her space, her world. When I was little, I think she used to go out more, but by the time I was old enough to remember, she mostly liked to stay in. Her routine was simple: She'd come home, have her drinks, and stay drunk until it was time to go to work the next day. That was just what she did.

Not everyone in my family was like that, though. My aunts, for example, were more parental than my own parents in many ways. They'd have a drink or two, but I never saw them drunk. They were too busy cooking, taking care of me and my cousins, and holding things together. They gave me a different kind of example—one I probably should have paid more attention to.

But at the end of the day, drinking was something that came naturally to me. And after prison, it became even more of a habit. Alcohol was my go-to. I was an alcoholic—100 percent.

I could stop. And sometimes, I did. But I always went back to it. It never felt like something I truly wanted to quit. It was part of my life, and that was that. But in the back of my head, there was always that little voice telling me, *You gotta stop.*

I knew what alcohol did to my family because I saw it firsthand. I hated it when my mom drank. My sister and I both did. We'd talk about it, how much we wished she'd stop. But the truth is, I was doing the same thing. Maybe in a different way, but it was still the same cycle playing out.

And then 2020 happened. The pandemic shut everything down, and suddenly, everyone was talking about their immune systems and how to stay healthy. That was when I started learning how bad alcohol could be for you. Health had never been more at the top of my mind.

Before that, I wasn't hip to the physical effects of alcohol. I knew what it did to people mentally—the way it changed their personalities, the way it made them act. But I never thought about what it was actually doing inside the body.

So I told myself, *Okay, we're gonna stop drinking to make our immune system stronger.* That was my logic at the time. It wasn't some deep realization about my drinking problem—it was just a practical decision. And besides, where was I even supposed to go to get drunk? Everything was closed. There were no bars, no parties, no get-togethers. It was a perfect excuse to stop.

Granted, I still drank a few times, but I cut back *a lot.*

Now, though, I don't drink at all.

The thing about alcohol was that it helped. Or at least, I thought it did. I had my OCD, ADHD, PTSD—so many things I was dealing with, and drinking made it all easier (or it felt like it did). When I drank, all of that faded into the background. It would go away, at least for a little while.

But I also used alcohol to socialize. That was a big part of it. Drinking made it easier to be around people, to have conversations and feel comfortable. But when everything shut down, when I wasn't around many people anymore, alcohol stopped making as much sense. It stopped being as fun. And that's when I had to sit with myself and ask the question: *Why do I want to feel this way?*

For the first time, I wasn't just drinking because it was there, or because it was part of the routine. I had to think about it. I had to sit with the feeling of being *drunk.*

And that's the thing. When I was drinking with people, it was often the thing that brought us together. It's easier to invite someone out for drinks than to invite them out to just . . . hang out. It's socially acceptable to go out for drinks. I don't think that's how it should be, but it's how it is.

Growing up where and how I did, I ended up doing a lot of socializing this way. We couldn't come together in other ways, and I wasn't even able to imagine what those other ways might be.

* * *

As I continued to learn to read, I discovered short stories. It sounds backward that I was reading novels before short stories but hey, I didn't know. It was incredible to me that there were books with many stories in them. I could pick them up, read one story, and then come back whenever I wanted.

And that was what I liked about *Point of Beauty*. It's a collection of fifty stories compiled by The Moth, which is a nonprofit collective that celebrates the art of storytelling. They hold storytelling slams where people tell stories—sometimes twenty minutes long!—without notes, and they also host a podcast featuring selected stories from the live events. Sometimes the stories are funny, sometimes they're sad, sometimes they're crazy, but they are always interesting.

That's what the book is like.

I read this book on my TikTok Lives, and I had so many people interacting with me. The book itself was a communal experience, and reading it live online was also a communal experience. Each story of *Point of Beauty* is different in its own way, but they all work together as a whole. The book resonates so much with me because it reminds me of my own online community.

This was something I could never have imagined coming together and *socializing* over. I couldn't imagine a book club when I was growing up in Pennsylvania.

And the theme of *Point of Beauty* resonates, too, of course. *True Stories of Holding On and Letting Go*. It's so much of what I've been learning: to let go of things that I'm attached to, but which don't serve me anymore.

Just like how I finally learned to let go of drinking.

12

READING IS THE QUESTION *WHY?*

The Four Agreements: A Practical Guide to Personal Freedom (1997), by Don Miguel Ruiz

When I read *The Four Agreements*, it affected me straight to my core. Now, a lot of the books I read when I first started reading had that kind of impact on me, but this one hit me everywhere. It completely knocked me into a new reality. It wove through my whole life, the core of who I was and who I am. It spoke not only to the changes I was making but the way I was making them.

I grew up with a lot of bad systems in place, a lot of superstitions and general ideas that I took for granted but couldn't back up. Stepping on a crack would break my mama's back, walking under a ladder was bad luck, a broken mirror meant the next seven years would be horrible, and Christmas was celebrated once a year by everyone in the world. We all grow up with those kinds of beliefs, things that shape our understanding of the world before we're even old enough to question them. They become part of the background, part of what we accept as *just the way things are.*

As I got older, I let go of some of those ideas and challenged some of them. I realized that some of them weren't true or at least weren't as important as I'd once thought. My mom's back never broke once after I'd stepped on a crack. But there were still so many givens in my head that I never even *thought* to challenge—especially before I started learning to read. They were too deeply ingrained. It wasn't that I *believed* them so much as I had never considered that I could *not* believe them.

In reading Don Miguel Ruiz's book, I learned that many of these "givens" were agreements.

Why agreements? Because they're not absolute laws of nature. You can ignore them, though you might regret it. They're deals we make with the world, sometimes without even realizing it. We assume that whatever we grow up believing or that our way of doing things is the truth, until one day we change our mind and see it differently. If we ever do.

I grew up knowing Christmas came once a year, always at the same time, always celebrated in more or less the same way. I thought it took over the whole world for that season. That was what Christmas was: red and green lights and Santa hats.

But when I got older, I found out there were people who didn't celebrate Christmas at all. To some people, December 25 is no different from any other day (except in many countries, more stores are closed). And yet, I still had this expectation in my head—this *agreement*—that Christmas is supposed to feel a certain way for everyone.

I had never *chosen* to believe that; the assumption was something I inherited. And there were so many other assumptions I have since come to question.

For example, I don't need to eat meat in my diet. That was crazy to realize. Everybody I knew ate meat—my family, my friends. It never even occurred to me that I *didn't* have to. So, when I started thinking about it, when I began asking myself if meat was even good for me, it threw me for a loop. *If I don't need to eat this, then why am I doing it?* There had to be a reason, right? But when I looked for one, I realized there was no reason I personally had to keep eating meat.

It wasn't the meat, or the coffee, or a consistent Christmas keeping me alive. Those weren't the things making the world turn.

If a friend I'm not that close with is getting married and I feel like I *have* to go, even though I don't want to, why is that? Is it because skipping their wedding is gonna kill me? Is it because going to weddings is the one thing keeping my heart beating?

No—at least, I doubt it.

It's because I made an agreement, somewhere along the way, that not going would make me a bad friend and, by extension, a bad person. But that agreement wasn't some universal truth—it was something I *decided* to believe, whether I realized it or not. It might be something I want to do, but it's not something I have to do.

And it goes deeper than that. Even things that seem objectively true aren't necessarily so.

Like my name. Is my name *really* Oliver? Does it *have* to be? That's just a title I was given, a word someone else decided for me. It's not the thing keeping me alive. If I wanted to, I could change it tomorrow, and I'd still wake up breathing.

I think, in retrospect, that's part of why I left Pennsylvania for California. Because I realized I didn't have to die under the same cold, cloudy skies I'd always lived under.

That realization wasn't something that hit me all at once. It wasn't some grand epiphany that came to me in a dream or in a moment of clarity. It was something quieter, something that crept up on me over time. I had always assumed—without ever saying it out loud—that I was going to live and die in the same place I was born. That was what people did. That was normal.

You grew where you were planted. You stayed near the people you knew. You worked, you lived, and you died in the same twenty-mile radius. It wasn't something I ever consciously agreed to. It was a fact of life, like the seasons changing or the sun rising.

But then, one day, I questioned it. One day, I sat with the idea and thought, *Wait—who said I have to? Who decided this for me?* And the answer was *no one.* No one had ever told me I couldn't leave. No one had ever said I was obligated to stay. But at the same time, no one had ever told me I *could* go, either. That was the tricky part.

When you start challenging things that fundamental, it's scary as hell. Because if that wasn't true—if I didn't have to die where I was born—then what *else* isn't true? What else in my life is something I accepted without question?

And that's when I realized: maybe a lot of things.

Maybe more than I was comfortable admitting.

How much of my life was built on things I never chose to believe? How many of my so-called truths were merely echoes of the people who came before me, passed down without anyone ever asking if they still made sense? What if everything I thought about the way things are was actually a collection of choices I had made without even knowing it?

That's where *The Four Agreements* helped me so much. It gave me a framework for understanding what was happening in my head. It explained things in a way that made sense. It made me realize that these "agreements" we make with ourselves aren't just things we pick up as kids and forget about. We're making new ones every single day. We're choosing what we believe, what we accept, what we think is normal—whether we realize it or not.

Some of those agreements are easy to see. The big ones, like "this is my home" or "this is the job I'll always have" or "this is who I am." But then there are the smaller ones, the ones we don't think about as much. The way we talk to ourselves. The way we react to criticism. The way we instinctively believe we're not good enough, or that we'll never change, or that life has to be hard.

We're attached to a lot of these beliefs, and that isn't always a bad thing. Some of them serve us. Some of them give us structure and comfort. But others? Others keep us stuck and make us believe we *can't* do things we're completely capable of doing.

And the thing is, we don't just make these agreements once and move on. Every single day, we reinforce them. Every day that you wake up and go through the motions of your same old routine and belief system, you're making the agreement all over again.

That's the part that took me the longest to understand. That you're *never* stuck. Even when it feels like you are. Even when it feels as though the choice has already been made for you. You can always wake up one day and decide to challenge everything.

That's what I did when I left Pennsylvania. It wasn't only about moving states. It was about proving to myself that my life wasn't set in stone. That I wasn't bound by some invisible contract I'd never signed. That I had the right to make new choices, to break old agreements, to decide—at any moment—that I could do something different.

And if I could do *that*, what else could I do?

Maybe I could be happy. Maybe I could be a good father, even if I never had one to show me how. Maybe I could forgive myself for all the times I fell short. Maybe I could learn to read.

Maybe I could stop believing that I was destined to be anything other than exactly who I decided to be.

Maybe I could put the cup down.

And pick something else up instead.

But because I understand that now doesn't mean I've thrown everything out. I'm still called Oliver—for now. I still show up to weddings, sometimes. Usually.

Not everything you're attached to is bad. I was lucky that my mom didn't raise me with crazy religious guilt, because I can only imagine how much harder it would've been to grow in this way if I had that weighing me down too. She let me figure things out for myself.

My problem wasn't religion. My problem was thinking I couldn't be anything other than what I already was.

And that's why looking at these agreements was so important to me. Because once I began questioning them, I saw how they actually *affected* me.

You can stop believing that skipping a wedding makes you a bad friend, but that doesn't mean everyone else will. And that's where the real challenge comes in. It's not only about *what you believe*, it's about how those beliefs interact with the world around you.

That's what I had to learn. It's not just about breaking old agreements. It's about deciding which new ones you want to make.

And I've experienced a lot of that.

I've learned that individuality is lonely. People don't always like it when you stop following the same rules they do. If you stop going to family functions, or stop eating meat, or stop drinking, people will *notice.* And they'll have opinions.

Sometimes they'll respect your choices. Sometimes they won't. And when they don't, you must ask yourself: *Does this matter to me? Is this an agreement I want to keep, or one I need to let go of?*

And that's a question I ask myself every single day.

Not only about myself, either. Once you start thinking this way, you can't *not* see it everywhere you look. It's like peeling back a layer of reality and realizing how much of what we take for granted is built on choices—conscious or not.

When I'm out in the world and I see someone who is beautiful, someone who's obviously put a lot of effort into their appearance, I wonder about the agreements they've made. *Why does it matter to them to look that way? How much work is it taking? Would they still think it was worth it if they asked themselves these kinds of questions?*

It's not that there's anything wrong with wanting to look good. But a lot of people don't ask themselves *why* they're doing it. Some people want to be attractive because it gives them control over something—over how they're perceived, over the way people treat them. Maybe looking good is their escape. Maybe it's the one thing in their life that feels predictable, something they can pour energy into when everything else feels chaotic.

And it's not only about appearances.

When I see one of those guys who's super into cars—one of those hyper-masculine types who's always working on his engine, making sure his exhaust is loud enough to shake the street—I think about the agreement *he's* made. *Does he seriously need to be working on his car all the time? Does he need it to be that loud?*

Maybe it's not about the car at all. Maybe it's a distraction, something to keep his mind occupied so he doesn't have to think about the things that actually scare him. Maybe he's afraid of not being seen as strong. Or of failing at something real. Maybe this version of himself—the one that fixes up his car, the one that leans into being *that guy*—is an agreement he's made with himself, one that keeps his eyes off whatever's lurking underneath.

But here's the thing: You can't tell people this kind of stuff.

You can't just walk up to someone and be like, *Hey, man, I think you're overcompensating for a deep-seated fear of vulnerability.*

That's not gonna go over well.

People don't hear your half-baked, armchair psychology and suddenly go, *Wow, thanks! I'm cured!* They assume you're being an asshole. Or that you're jealous. Or that you don't get it.

And the truth is, maybe you *don't* get it. Maybe they *do* know why they're doing what they're doing, and they don't care. Maybe they've made peace with their agreements, even if you wouldn't make the same ones.

I remember growing up watching pop stars on TV, and it seemed as if they were larger than life. Like they weren't ever gonna fade. They weren't gonna get old, or messy, or caught up in scandals. They were always *there*, constant, untouchable. And at the time, I didn't think about what it *meant* to be them. I didn't think about the reality behind the image.

Looking back, it's obvious how much of that belief—the idea that these people were somehow different from the rest of us—was just another agreement. One we all bought into. And that agreement still exists today.

When people want to be famous, when they dream about being rappers or pop stars or actors, a lot of the time, they aren't even thinking about what that life would be like. They're thinking about the *idea* of it.

They're thinking about the music videos, the awards, the magazine covers. They're not thinking about the exhaustion, the pressure, the lack of privacy. They're not thinking about how it might in reality *feel* for *them*.

Because at the end of the day, big celebrities still get hangovers. They still get food poisoning and all the ugly symptoms that go along with that. They still brush their teeth and take out the trash and fall asleep watching TV. They have problems, breakups, arguments with friends, financial juggling, and all the other trappings of a regular life. Like, they're normal people underneath it all.

But when people imagine being famous, they don't think about *any* of that.

They don't think about the fact that they are making *agreements* every day to be and stay who they are. We only see the characters they play, the songs they sing, the interviews they do. That's all. We don't stop to ask *why* they do what they do. Why they dress a certain way, or talk the way they do in interviews; why they keep pushing forward even when it looks like they have everything they could possibly want. We take it at face value—as if it's all inevitable, all part of the script. But none of it really is.

Half the time, we don't even stop to wonder why *we* do what *we* do. We wake up, go about our day, follow the same routines, act out the roles we've accepted for ourselves—all without questioning where those choices came from. Without asking whether they're *actually* choices, or habits we've never broken. Agreements we've never stopped to reevaluate.

And that's exactly what I found so impactful about *The Four Agreements*, and about reading in general.

I've read a lot of self-help books by now. And they're different from fiction, of course. But what both genres do is present information to you, one way or another, and leave it up to you to decide what to do with it. And once you start thinking that way—once you recognize those same invisible forces in yourself want to attach to the ideas that resonate—it becomes harder to just *be* without wondering *why*.

And then things get a lot more interesting.

13

READING IS FOR FATHERS

The Pivot Year: 365 Days to Become the Person You Truly Want to Be (2023), by Brianna Wiest

My relationship with my father was complicated growing up. That's one more of the clichés I lived. He wasn't around much when I was a kid, but at the same time, he was. Just not in the way a father usually is—not in the way where he's there to teach you things, to guide you, to check in on how your day went. But he wasn't completely absent, either. He existed somewhere in between, living in this strange halfway place, present but never fully engaged.

His side of the family is Jamaican, and they had a communal way of living. It wasn't like the standard setup, where a household consists of the parents and the kids, apart from the rest of the extended family. Instead, everyone was together—one big unit in one small place.

My aunts, uncles, and cousins—they all lived in the same house, coming and going as they pleased. The door was always open, figuratively and sometimes literally. People popped in and out all the time, whether they lived there or not. If you needed a meal, you came by. If you wanted to see someone, you didn't call first—you just showed up. It wasn't exactly a home; it was a meeting place, a hub, a space where family just *was*.

That was where I went to see my father. But it wasn't like I was going to *his* house—it was simply where he happened to be. When I got dropped off there, for his shared custody time, I wasn't being left with *him*. I was being left with *family*. And who that meant on any given day was impossible to predict.

And throughout all this, I was kinda on my own to figure it out. I have a sister that I was raised with, but she's almost a decade older than me, so we didn't have a lot in common the way we would have if we'd been closer in age. I also have two step-siblings, an older sister and younger brother, my dad's from another relationship. So, despite having siblings, I was on my own with navigating all this.

A lot of the time, my mom would barely slow the car down when she dropped me off at my dad's house. She'd pull up, drop me, and be gone before anyone saw her. Or, I guess, before she had to see anyone.

It wasn't like she was handing me off to my father directly, making sure I was in his care before I was out of her sight. She was dropping me into the mix, knowing that somebody—an aunt, a cousin, an uncle—would take me in and I'd be absorbed into the other side of my family. Sometimes my dad was there, and sometimes he wasn't. Maybe he'd be gone for the whole weekend, off doing whatever he was doing, and I wouldn't see him at all. Other times, he'd be there, but not really *there*. He might be busy, caught up in his own world, drifting in and out of conversations, present in the way a piece of furniture is—something you notice but don't interact with much.

That was how it was. I never questioned it. I didn't feel abandoned or neglected, because I wasn't alone. My aunts made sure I ate, made sure I was good. I'd spend the time hanging out with my cousins, playing, getting lost in the shuffle of a big, bustling household. It wasn't bad—not in the usual way people think when they hear about a father not being there. I wasn't left to fend for myself. I wasn't unloved. I was part of something bigger, something that wasn't centered around *me*.

But looking back, I can see that while I was surrounded by people, I wasn't necessarily getting what a son is supposed to get from a father. My dad wasn't *raising* me. He wasn't showing me how to navigate the world or passing down lessons in any real way. He was just *around*—an occasional presence in a house that belonged to everyone, never solely mine.

And when you grow up like that, you don't notice what's missing. There's no context for it. You accept things as they are. That was my normal. It wasn't until much later that I realized what I didn't have.

My cousins and I ended up feeling more like siblings because of the setup at that house, but one of my cousins, in particular, took me under his wing. He was older, so he taught me how to dress, how to be more mature, how to talk to girls, stuff like that. He also taught me to watch out for myself, how to be careful about who I trusted, how to move around the streets a little better. I didn't have any older boys or a dad around, so it was nice that he helped me out like that.

I thought it was cool, you know? I always wanted to see my cousin—he was like a brother to me. Since he didn't live with me, going to see my dad always felt like stepping into another world with a whole alternative family. One where I had siblings and lots of hustle and bustle in the house all the time. I'd walk in, say hi to the older people—my grandma, my aunts, whoever was there—and they'd barely look up before saying, "He's upstairs." This was always the routine.

I was at that house a lot, but it never felt like enough. Sometimes once a week, sometimes once a month. Other times, especially in the summer, I'd stay there for two or three weeks straight, but I wasn't only there for my dad. I was mostly there for my cousin.

Most of the time, nobody even knew I was coming. My mom would drop me off, and I'd either ring the doorbell or walk right in. They'd open the door, looking at me like, *Oh, what are you doing here?*—half surprised, half unbothered. Being Jamaican, they were direct about it, too, like, *Nobody told us you were coming.* And as a kid, I didn't have an answer. I'd shrug, stand there, and wait for them to move aside so I could go inside. It was never a big deal, though. They'd let me in, point upstairs, and that was that.

And I remember it so clearly—walking up to my cousin's room, stepping inside, and immediately entering his world. He was always doing something. Maybe he was listening to music, drawing, cleaning his shoes, putting an outfit together. He was that type of person—always in motion, always onto something. I'd barely get through the door before he'd glance up and go, "Oh, what up?"

And just like that, everything shifted, and I was in a whole new world.

It was like stepping into a different reality—even though it was only ten minutes away from where my mom lived. One second, I was a kid dropped off at my dad's family's house; the next, I was part of whatever my cousin had going on. "You got some clothes?" he'd ask. And if I didn't, no problem—he'd toss me an outfit. "Here, put this on. We're going to a party."

I was eleven years old. He was thirteen, fourteen. And we were hopping on bikes, heading to a party like it was nothing. That was the energy he had—he wasn't the type to sit around playing video games or waiting for the day to pass. He had plans. If he was going to the barbershop, I was going too. "Go get twenty bucks from your dad," he'd say.

And yeah, sometimes my dad was there, sometimes he wasn't. If he was, he was usually up on the third floor, lying in bed or doing his own thing. One thing he would definitely not be doing, let me tell you, was *reading a book*. I never saw him read. I'm not sure if either of my parents can read.

I'd go up there, poke my head in, and he'd look at me, confused. "What are you doing here?"

"My mom dropped me off," I'd say.

He'd pause, as if he was recalibrating his whole day. Like he had plans, and now here I was, thrown into them without warning. But after a second, he'd sigh and go, "All right."

And I'd be like, "Can I get twenty dollars?"

He'd hand it over, no questions asked. That was it. That was our interaction for the day.

Then I was back downstairs, back in my cousin's world. We'd get haircuts, ride our bikes across town, end up at some friend's house where they were talking about school or girls or random nonsense. And even though these were my cousin's friends, they felt like mine too. Every time I came around, it was like I'd never left.

"Oh, what up? You back?"

"Yeah, got here today."

"Bet you coming to the party tonight?"

And that was how it went. I wasn't just visiting—I was stepping in and out of a life that wasn't exactly mine but felt like home every time I returned.

I owe my cousin a lot for everything he did. He helped me grow, taking the role of a father figure in some ways, as weird as that sounds.

Lots of people did, in the end. It was a house full of people, and I picked up lessons from them along the way. And some of that was great. But I know I missed out on something. I can't even define what it was, but I know that I wanted more from my dad.

Now I'm a father myself. And, man, it's tough.

Sometimes I find myself staring at my son, and I start crying. I wonder—*did my dad look at me like this?* Ever? I don't even know how to explain it. It's an emotion I haven't fully processed yet. I don't think I've even had the chance. I'm still so busy beating myself up, trying not to be the father I was raised by. And I'm here, every day, doing everything I can to be there for my son. But I still catch myself thinking—*am I here enough?*

It's strange, though, being an adult now. I've got my own personal issues to deal with. And I realize maybe my dad had his own too. I mean, he must have. His relationship with my mom didn't work out—it was even pretty ugly sometimes—but he still made time to see me and have me be part of his/our extended family. Maybe that was harder for him to work out than I realized. Maybe he couldn't explain things to me, things I'm not even aware of, just like I can't always put my thoughts into words now.

He never told me he loved me. That was messed up. Never gave me hugs, never kissed me on the forehead. I don't know if he ever even shook my hand, to be honest. There wasn't a lot of affection; feeling loved would have gone a long way toward making me feel worthy of the good things the world had to offer. It might have given me more inspiration to succeed in school, to make my parents proud.

Not that I'm blaming it all on them—so many things had to go wrong to put me in the place I ended up, but anyone can see that security and love at home would have helped keep me from getting lost in the shuffle.

My partner, Anne, has a child from a previous relationship, and we had a son together soon after moving to California. After everything I didn't get, I make sure that both those boys get the kind of care I never had a thousand times over. I'll kiss them, hug them, tell them I love them every single day for as long as I'm here. I'll encourage their every little success and help them when they fall. I know there will be times when they're older that they'll do things I don't agree with, but I've vowed to myself to make sure they feel loved no matter what. Even when they're fifty. Because I didn't have that, and I know what it's like to want it.

The thing is, I grew up not even realizing what a father was supposed to be. I thought the way my dad was, was just how dads were. Guys who didn't say or do much. I had no blueprint. And so I'm making it up as I go.

At the same time, my dad did give me a blueprint of sorts—but in reverse. He showed me exactly what not to do. So now, I take the good things he did—like when he gave me money for the movies or took me out occasionally—and I do those things. But I also add in everything he didn't do. If he never told me he loved me, I make sure my kids hear it every day. If he didn't pick me up when he said he would, I make sure I always show up. Because that was the worst part: He wasn't there. And I spent years blaming my mom for it.

She never blamed him, though. I'd hear her on the phone with him, arguing, and sink inside. *She's pissing him off,* I'd think. *It's her fault.* She'd made him mad and then he wouldn't want to see me. Or he wouldn't be so nice when he did. But she never put it on him. She never said, "Your dad is a piece of crap." She would say, "Oliver, he's not perfect." That was all.

"He's not perfect, and I don't know what to tell you."

Now, looking back, I get it. That was an incredible act of love. She had to be mad at him too. It must have been frustrating for her not to be able to count on him for help or co-parenting, especially when I got into trouble. It would be tempting to want to snatch all the parenting credit for herself and tell me he was a dog, but she knew whatever he was, I was half him. And she loved me.

I don't think my dad didn't love me. I think he had his own struggles. Struggles he never talked about, never admitted to, maybe never even fully understood himself. I think he carried things he didn't know how to put down. And when you don't know how to put something down, you end up handing it off to the next person without even meaning to.

I don't want to do that to my kids.

I *won't* do that to my kids.

Because one day, they're going to grow up. One day, they'll see me in a way they can't see me now. Right now, I'm just *Dad.* The guy who picks them up, the guy who makes the rules, the guy who's always supposed to know what he's doing. But one day, they'll realize I'm just a person. A man who's made mistakes. A man who tried, who loved them more than they'll ever understand, but who still, inevitably, got things wrong. And when that day comes—when they come to me with their own version of this story, with their own hurts—will I be ready to accept it?

That scares me.

Because no matter how hard I try, I know I'll fall short in some way. No parent gets it entirely right. That's the truth. And one day, I might hear my kids say the words that would shatter me: "Dad, you weren't there for me the way I needed."

And when that happens—because at some point, in some way, it *will*—what will I do? Will I sit back, take a breath, push aside my own shame and guilt, and say, "You're right. I wish I had done better. I did everything I could, but I'm sorry for the things I missed"?

Or will I get defensive? Will I do what so many parents do—list everything I ever did for them, all the sacrifices, all the sleepless nights, all the ways I tried so hard to be different from my own father—and tell them they should be grateful? Will I turn their pain into my own and make them feel like they have no right to it?

I don't want to be that parent.

Actually, I guess you could call my difficult upbringing an advantage as far as knowing what *not* to do.

I want to be someone they can talk to about *anything*, someone who listens without judgment. Someone who doesn't make excuses and encourages them to take responsibility too. Someone who tells them the truth—even when it hurts. I want them to know that just because I tried my best doesn't mean I always got it right. And I hope that if I can show them *that* kind of honesty, they won't be afraid to show it back.

Because the truth is, love isn't about being perfect. It's about being *there*. It's about making sure that when my kids look back at their childhood, they'll know—without a doubt—that I cared. That I tried. That I was always willing to own up to my mistakes.

That I was human.

And that being human was never an excuse to stop trying to be better.

And I want them to *know* that. I don't want them to have to piece it together.

Because that's another thing I never got. No one ever sat me down and told me who they were inside. No one ever said, "This is what happened to me. This is why I am the way I am."

I wish my dad had done that. I wish he had told me his story—who he was, what he went through. The pain he carried. I think if he had, I would have understood him. And maybe—maybe—I wouldn't have spent so much of my life trying to figure it out on my own. I know so little about him. I don't know where he grew up, or *how* he grew up. I don't know what he did for a living, I don't know his age. All I know is his name, and whatever I've seen with my own two eyes.

I called him on the day my son was born. My grandma had passed not too long ago—his mom—and he was going through that. And I was going through a lot too. I had recently had a child. I didn't know how to be a dad. I was lost.

So, I called him that day, just kind of . . . I don't know. Just to talk.

But it was the same as always. Nothing new. It was like he had nothing to give. I was trying to tell him what I was going through, how I was changing, how everything felt so overwhelming, and he simply—he wasn't hearing me. It was like he didn't know *how* to hear me. He doesn't know me as an adult with a child of my own. He still sees me as the little boy who slipped through his fingers.

That's how he talks to me—like I'm still eight years old. Like I'm still some obedient kid. I swore at some point on the call, and he told me, *You don't talk to your dad like that. You don't speak that way.* And I was thinking, *What?* I'm a grown man. I'm thirty-four years old. I have a child. And you want to tell me how to speak?

I hadn't called to be scolded. I'd called because I wanted to know him. To understand him. But I don't think we know how to communicate. We never built that relationship. There's no foundation. And so, when we talk, it's like we're speaking two different languages. I haven't spoken to him since that day.

Becoming a father not only changed my life—it forced me to see my own childhood in a way I never had before. It's one thing to feel the weight of what you lacked growing up, to carry it with you without realizing how heavy it is. It's another thing entirely to hold your child in your arms, to look into their eyes and suddenly recognize, with a sharp and painful clarity, everything you should have had but didn't. The presence that should have been there. The comfort. The safety. The love that wasn't questioned, wasn't earned, wasn't something you had to wonder about.

And that's when I realized—my dad wasn't going to change. Not because he couldn't, but because he didn't know how. Or maybe he never wanted to. Brianna Wiest writes in *The Pivot Year* that growth is a decision. That change isn't something that just happens to you—it's something you must choose. And in that moment, I understood that my father had made his choice a long time ago. He had chosen distance. He had chosen silence. He had chosen whatever was easier for him, instead of what I needed.

But now it was my turn to choose.

In *The Pivot Year*, Wiest encourages her readers to let go of the past, find strength now, and be kind to yourself in the process. I was and am trying hard to make sure that's what I do. Not only can I release the things that did me wrong in the past, but I can also make sure that I take care of my*self* now the way I wish I'd been cared for then—and even more importantly, make sure that my boys have what I didn't. As encouraged by *The Pivot Year*, I have aligned with my purpose, and it is my intention to move forward with it in every action.

Because I could feel it, that pull, that legacy, that cycle trying to repeat itself. The kind of fatherhood where you stay disconnected, where you let pride or fear or whatever excuse you tell yourself keep you from showing up. It would be easy to become that. To keep my walls up. To hold myself back. To love from a distance instead of leaning in, being vulnerable, being *there*. But love isn't just something you feel. It's something you do. It's in the showing up. It's in the staying. It's in the quiet moments that no one else sees, the ones that my sons will grow up knowing, without question, were real.

I don't know what kind of father I am yet. I'm still figuring it out. But I know what kind of father I *won't* be. And maybe that's how it starts. Maybe breaking the cycle is about deciding that the past doesn't get to decide for you.

I don't want to be the kind of father that my dad was.

And I love him. I do. But I don't know if I'll ever know him.

And that's the thing, isn't it? That's why people write books. To tell their stories. So that the next generation doesn't have to guess. So that when my own son grows up, he won't have to wonder who I was or what I felt. He'll know. And he'll be able to take that knowledge, carry it forward, and do even better.

Because that's the goal, right? To break the cycle. To build something better. To leave behind more than just memories—but lessons.

A legacy.

A story worth telling.

14

READING IS THERAPY

Lighter: Let Go of the Past, Connect with the Present, and Expand the Future (2022), by Yung Pueblo

GIVEN EVERYTHING I'VE SHARED, you can probably tell that therapy has been pretty important in my life. Not because I'm so obviously healed or anything, but because it's a lot to sort through. I have spent a lot of time and energy and worked hard to cope with it all. To learn the tools to use to prevent OCD taking over my life, though certainly I still have my moments. To slow down and not let ADHD run me. To breathe and not live in the reactivity of PTSD.

And also, to accept my parents for who they were and are. And besides real therapy, I've gotten so much out of reading as a therapeutic outlet as well.

The intrusive and twisted thoughts caused by OCD resulted in me thinking constantly, for years, about my mother's death. With each time I thought about it came pain, fear, and dread. Once I started reading, I was able to learn how to use those thoughts as a place to explore ideas instead of being overwhelmed by them. I could see that my mind was telling me a story, so that I could work through these emotions instead of agonizing over them.

I imagined how I'd feel to lose my mom—the gut-wrenching sorrow and my heart with an empty spot forever. Miserable, yes, but I saw it as a story now. Saw the sadness, the grief, felt the surge of shock and pain. And with that imagining as "prep," I was able to find some sort of acceptance of something that will one day come. To accept the cycle of life at the very least, not live every day being haunted by the idea of something so terrible rocketing into my life and devastating me in, literally, unimaginable ways. I don't mean any of this callously.

Thankfully, my mother is alive and well in North Carolina and I hope she is for a very long time. But when that day comes, I hope that I've come far enough in my reading and mental health to handle the pain with acceptance and grace rather than it feeling like the horrible conclusion to uncontrolled, intrusive thinking.

Now that I feel more capable of controlling my mind, you know, as much as I can, I'm far more calm and able to compose myself and figure out what to do. When people are dying, or chaotic things are happening in the world and on the news and internet, I am more prepared. I have worked out those muscles. It happens, it may happen, it did happen.

In books, in stories, you can find every emotion. You can feel happy, carried away by a love story; you can feel terror and grief; you can laugh out loud. Before I learned to read, every time I had an emotion, it would paralyze me. I couldn't see it coming. I couldn't recognize the pattern. And then it would hit me, and I'd be like, *What is this? Why do I feel this way?* Without a blueprint, I had no idea how to handle it. Or where to take it.

One of my more recent reads was a book titled *Lighter*. I found it to be so helpful as I started to process the effect reading was having on me. It helped with my sobriety as well. The book has practices—actual things you can do day to day—which is a huge benefit for me. I'm still not at a real high reading level, so absorbing a cloud of ideas all at once can sometimes be overwhelming—though I look forward to the day when it won't be. But this book has real tools, things I can apply right now. It has given me hope and clarity and feels like a companion in all this change.

Lighter is, in some ways, about letting go of emotional baggage. Not attaching all your shit to everything in your life. This allows you to live in the here and now. And while I found myself unable to stop fixating on the future and the inevitable thing I feared, I was able to accept that the *fear* was what was happening *now*. The *thing* itself was not. My mother's death was not happening. I was simply in a moment, with fear. That realization helped me be more present.

I've seen my mom die a thousand times in my mind throughout the past twenty years, but why do I feel more comfortable with it (or at least less terrified) now? I think it's because reading has helped me manage my responses to fear. I can see how much I share with the people and characters I read about. Even when I think I haven't got anything in common with someone in a book, by the end, I understand them. I know, now, how to stay tapped into the beauty and joy of life in every situation. I know how to keep happiness at my core.

Lighter also allowed me to stop my mind from ping-ponging so frantically from place to place. I could calm down and go with the flow. Reading it was like a meditation.

One of the ways I tackled this was that I'd pick someone who I disliked or even hated. I'd picture them in my head and tell myself, *Okay—now love them.* Not always an easy task. Trying to look at others through the lens of love has helped me, and I can only do that because I've gained empathy by reading about other people's experiences, real or not real. If I keep sitting with hate, then that's my problem. I'm the one who has the hostile feelings, not the person I'm obsessing about. I was holding that destructive emotion in my body, heart, and mind. And it was corroding me.

Until I filled the space with empathy. And to do that, I had to imagine it.

Today I focus on positivity. But I can't control everyone else. To change means separating myself from some people who still continue the same old negative conversation, but now, I'm out of that cycle. Now, I have more to say.

It would be easy for me to pity myself for the way my growth has separated me from others I used to know. But the truth is it feels *better* to live empathetically. Love is an incredible feeling. Joy is infectious. It might not make hippies of everyone, but to share a little love and to change a few minds is incredibly fulfilling.

It's a gift to be able to imagine the feelings others are having. I remember being a kid when my mom used to tell me that she was experiencing something—I wasn't able to feel it. Couldn't empathize at all.

That broke me for a while. Made me think something was wrong with me at home too, when school had already confirmed how different and bad I was. How much I lacked.

I accepted that as a child. The way children do. Sometimes, my mom would think I was being ignorant or mean, but she didn't understand *me*, either. I was learning to deal. To cope.

And then I had all those intrusive thoughts. I thought of her lying in a casket. Life without her. How lost I'd be. I spent my young life fearing death—my own, the death of people I loved . . . just death.

But then, I remember being a kid and realizing she actually *didn't* live like I did. Now I know this fixation on the death of a parent to be a common fixation of people—especially children—with OCD, which is something else I've managed to explore through therapy and reading. At the time, though, I was like, *What is wrong with me?*

I remember being at a funeral once and seeing everybody crying. Yet I felt numb. Empty. Didn't care and couldn't feel what everyone was so obviously suffering with. And I knew that they would think there was something weird going on with me if they noticed. So, I stared at the lights to make my eyes water. It made me feel like such an outsider, flawed. My context, my world, everything told me *I* was wrong.

I felt guilty. I wanted to feel what they felt. But now that I've begun to read, I'm not controlled by those thoughts anymore.

To me, one of the most interesting things about looking at this part of my past through the lens of reading is that now I notice all the different ways I've learned things over the years.

There's passive learning, which is how I learned everything for a while. It's not conscious, it's repeating patterns and mimicking what you see in your world.

Then there is active learning, which is how you learn in school (in theory) or through reading. It's going out of your way for knowledge. I had only done passive learning for so much of my life. I didn't use my voice because I didn't know I could.

When I started reading, I began making a conscious effort to choose what takeaways I liked from a particular book, what pieces resonated with me, and what parts made me want to change and adapt. In a way, it's like I was re-parenting myself. I was finally able to give myself the support I needed but never had in certain areas of my life. My mom tried to give me her world, her understanding, her ways of coping with life. But it just never clicked for me. I had figured out my own ways, on my own.

Which makes sense. Just because she's my mom doesn't mean we have the same worldview. No one has the *exact* same worldview or perspective as anyone else, because we're all individuals. Now that I can access many different points of view, I can take the parts I want and build my own ways of seeing. Since I'm learning from so many varied minds, I'm creating a combination that is unique to me. I'm realizing that everything in my life before now was imitation.

Now that I can read, there are some simple life questions that I'm only now getting the answers to.

When I read, I have a safe place to ask questions and to get answers. There were important questions I was asking as a kid. Kids' questions might seem silly, but that's the way we learn about the world when we're young. We need to ask questions and get answers from many places to build a strong foundation.

I was hanging out in my neighborhood one time and a friend came up to me and said he had started going to church. He told me that I needed to go to church too, or else I'd die and go to hell. I didn't know how to react; I didn't even know what hell was. I didn't know what church was. None of it. I was maybe five or something. He said that the devil was going to come and give me the 666 mark. I didn't know what that meant, but I was super scared of it. He was telling me this because someone had told him.

I remember being scared and then running home with my heart pounding. I had never felt anything like that in my life. I wasn't simply scared, like when you step out in the street and almost get clipped. I was scared like . . . on another level. My breathing was messed up, my blood felt hot and cold.

At the time I didn't know it was anxiety. I didn't know I was mid–panic attack. I didn't know a thing. I was getting dropped with death, hell, and the devil with his pitchfork on a random afternoon. I ran home, went up to my mother, and said, "Mom, did you know you could die?"

She just looked at me. It's like she was saying, *Oh, he doesn't know* in her mind because she hesitated long enough to scare me.

"Yes," she told me after a moment. "But you don't need to think about it now. That won't be happening for a long, long time."

I remember leaving the house after that, walking out the front door, and having the sun hit me. I began to calm down. To forget, even. As a kid, you can't hold onto thoughts in the same way as when you're an adult. You don't replay things that much. My OCD sometimes made my thoughts loop, but in this case, my ADHD kicked in! I saw the squirrels, took in everything around me, and . . . let it go. I moved on.

But unfortunately, every time the topic of death came up—in a movie, in conversation—I would get sucked right back to that place. I'd start thinking about death. And every time, I would think about my mom dying.

Nobody answered the question of *what is death* for me. It was an important part of my existence. I was supposed to find that out. I was supposed to have somebody who had knowledge to give me about this difficult subject. Now obviously there's no perfect answer—nobody knows exactly what happens after we die, of course—but even still, I could have been given an understanding. Something comforting, maybe. Or at least the facts, not just a dismissal.

And since I was so used to taking what I was told and having to roll with it, not having the ability to intentionally or passively explore other ideas, I lived with this uncomfortable lack of knowledge. Death will freak any kid out, but damn.

My mother's fear of the unknown, as well as her avoidance of and unwillingness to think about ideas that were scary, were all issues I inherited. They pushed me to a place where I didn't learn what I needed to learn. They definitely informed my life moving forward: how I confronted my own fears, and my thoughts about education.

Mastering the art of avoidance when your world is actively not leading you is dangerous. I wasn't being proactive; I wasn't seeking out. I was learning to avoid, when at that time what could have helped me was to pursue, not avoid.

Now that I can read pretty well (which is still so wild to me), I'm able to get some answers to these questions. Honestly, can you imagine how hard that was at thirty-two? To finally step back and realize that reading could have been the antidote for all that fear and panic.

That's why it's been so hard to accept these things.

And it's reading that gave me that. It showed me that I could heal the deep cuts I needed to, to grow and change. It showed me that change was possible and positive.

But I kept asking, and soon I didn't even know myself anymore.

Now that I was without my habits for calming down—drinking, weed—I didn't know what to do. I thought that I'd try something new. I tried exercising more and eating differently, attempting to get in the best shape of my life. One day after working out, I thought I'd read a little bit.

For the first time, because of my ability to read, I can harness things in my life and control them in a measured way.

Therapy is all about seeing yourself more clearly. It's all about seeing the reality of yourself and then coming up with a way to be better going forward and to heal from what's come before. Reading does the same thing.

Reading can help you to see it. And then let it go.

15

READING IS 100

The Giving Tree (1964), by Shel Silverstein
Fish in a Tree (2015), by Lynda Mullaly Hunt

When I made the decision to read one hundred books in a year, it wasn't because I had some deep love for books yet. At that point, I'd barely read any. And it wasn't because I had a clear vision of what I would gain from it. It was because I understood fitness. That was my framework for everything, the one thing in my life that made sense. And if I could apply that same structure, that same discipline, to reading, I was willing to trust that maybe it could change me in ways I couldn't yet understand. Same as what happens when you start taking your fitness seriously.

I had built my life around dodging the need to read, finding ways to get by. And for the longest time, I told myself it didn't matter. I didn't need to read. I could live without it. I had other strengths, other ways of getting through the world.

But deep down, I knew something was missing. I just didn't know how to approach it. Reading wasn't something you could suddenly be good at. And, frankly, the longer you don't learn how to read, the more impossible it seems. There was no simple fix, no switch to flip that would make it easier. And that's when I began thinking about fitness.

Before I got into working out, I didn't understand it, either. When I was a kid, I thought fitness was mainly about muscles, about looking a certain way. Trying to look good for girls. But once I began working out, I realized it was so much more than that. It was about taking care of my heart, my lungs, my body. It was about endurance, feeling stronger, and waking up with more energy. It was about my mind as much as my muscles.

That realization changed everything for me. And I wondered—if fitness could do that for my body, what could reading do for my mind?

That's how I decided to approach it. I wouldn't try to comprehend everything right away. I wouldn't analyze themes or memorize details. I needed to build the habit, to get in shape with my reading the same way I had gotten in shape with my body. Every chapter was a rep. Every book was a set. I didn't care if I understood everything perfectly; I needed to do the work.

And just as with fitness, the first steps were brutal. I could barely get through a few pages without feeling exhausted. My focus would slip, my mind would wander, and I'd have to force myself to keep going. But I kept showing up. I kept picking up the books, turning the pages, even when it felt impossible.

Before I realized how it applied to reading, I knew this about discipline: the longer you avoid something, the tougher it is to start. Just like how skipping workouts makes it more difficult to get back in shape, avoiding reading had made it harder for my brain to process words. I had spent years thinking reading was something I wasn't good at, when in reality, the "reading" part of my brain was out of shape.

So, I treated it like a fitness journey. A New Year's resolution—except instead of lifting weights or running miles, I was lifting words off a page and running through stories. Priority number one was showing up, day after day, and putting in the time.

I realized that so much of life is like that. It's not always about natural talent or instant understanding—it's about practice. We expect to get better at things just by wanting to, but that's not how it works. We must exercise our skills, emotions, and habits. We must train our minds the way we train our bodies.

I had never thought about that before. That everything we do—our relationships, emotions, and our ability to focus—could be worked on, strengthened, built up better over time. I had always assumed that if I wasn't naturally good at something, it just wasn't for me. But that wasn't true. I just hadn't put in the reps.

I started thinking about my life differently. If I wasn't smiling as much as I used to, maybe my happiness was out of shape. If I struggled to control my emotions, maybe I needed to work on them like a muscle. And if I couldn't read, it wasn't because I wasn't meant to—it was because I had never trained my brain to do it.

And the more I read, the more I saw the results. Like working out, it didn't happen overnight. But I felt it. My focus got better. My understanding deepened. Eventually, like a runner's high, I began to enjoy the process.

Reading wasn't just about the books themselves. It was about unlocking something inside myself. It was about proving that I could change, that I could grow, that I wasn't limited by what I had always believed about myself.

It was more than a challenge. It was a necessary transformation.

And then, I began seeing gains, learning. Slowly, painfully. I stumbled through books, probably missing stuff that was easy for most people. And at first, it was frustrating as hell. Reading felt like trying to lift weights that were way too heavy for me. I'd get through a paragraph and feel exhausted. You know when you read a paragraph and, at the end, you realize you didn't retain any of it? For me, that happened every single time I read anything, even if I *did* know the words. My brain wasn't used to it. It wasn't wired for this—or so I thought.

And then, in 2022, I did something that should have been impossible for me. I told myself I was going to read one hundred books in a single year. A hundred. Not five. Not ten. A *hundred.*

When I say that out loud, it still sounds insane. I mean, not long before that, I had barely read *one* book cover to cover. But I wasn't thinking about the number itself. I wasn't thinking about the books, or what they meant, what I would learn, or even about reaching the goal, and what that would mean. I was thinking about reading the way I thought about fitness.

See, working out was the one thing I understood. I knew what it was like to push myself in the gym, to train my body even when I didn't feel like it. I knew that if you lift a little more each day, if you run a little farther, if you keep showing up, your body *adapts.* You get stronger. And I wondered—what if my brain worked the same way? What if I had spent my whole life assuming I *couldn't* enjoy reading, when in fact, I had just never trained for it, so it was a muscle that got sore quick?

I began treating individual books like workouts. Every day, I picked one up, even if I didn't want to. Even if I was tired. Even if I felt stupid or embarrassed. I forced myself to do the lift. To sit with the discomfort. To get through a few more pages than I did the day before. Sometimes, I'd literally do both "reading workouts" and physical workouts at the same time: listening to audiobooks or reading between reps.

Some books made me feel like I was drowning in words I didn't understand. But the more I read, the stronger I got. My brain was keeping up. Words didn't seem so foreign anymore. They were making sense. I was actually making sense *of them.*

It was like my mind had been locked in a cage for years, and now, finally, it was learning how to move.

When you work out every day, you see results in unexpected places. Suddenly, stairs don't feel as steep. You didn't even realize they had felt steep before. You wake up with more energy, when you didn't even know that you were tired before. Your body moves differently, feels different. Reading was the same way. It wasn't just about reading, either—it was about *how I thought.* I understood people better. I understood myself better. I asked better questions. I saw connections in places I never had before.

And then something even crazier happened: I realized I was genuinely *enjoying* it.

I started seeing books the way I saw gym equipment—tools to make me better. Every single book introduced me to a new way of thinking, a new way of seeing the world. And not every book would be the same—like not all exercise machines are the same.

I read *The Giving Tree* and had to sit with it for months before I fully understood what it was saying. I read *The Alchemist* and thought about destiny and manifestation in ways I never had before. I read books on history, self-improvement, philosophy. Some were easy, some were damn near impossible, but every single one stretched my mind in a way I had never felt before.

One hundred books. That number still amazes me. But what's even more amazing is how different I was by the end of it.

Because reading a hundred books wasn't just about checking titles off a list. It was about proving to myself that I could do something I never thought I could. It was about learning *how* to learn.

Discipline. It was about showing up for myself, day after day, even when it was hard. Even when I wanted to quit.

Some books changed the way I saw the world. Lots of them confirmed things I had already felt but never had the words for. Some made me uncomfortable. Others made me feel understood for the first time. And some, honestly, weren't that great—but even those taught me something and helped me grow. I was beginning to have taste in books! Opinions.

By the end of that year, reading wasn't just something I did—it was part of who I was. And that was the biggest change of all.

Because once you see yourself as a reader, as someone who learns, as someone who grows, you realize something: there's no limit to what you can do next. When I set out to read one hundred books in a year, I wasn't thinking about the outcome. I wasn't strategizing about what I would gain from it or mapping out some master plan to become a better version of myself. It was a journey without a destination. I knew that I had seen people commit to things before—things they didn't fully understand at first—and by the end, they had transformed. I saw people run every day for a year, post about it online, talk about how much their life had changed, how their bodies felt stronger, how their minds felt clearer. And I thought, maybe reading could be like that. Maybe if I committed, without knowing what the end result would be, something inside me would change.

I had no idea what was coming. But I went into it with a mindset that felt familiar. I wasn't reading for comprehension, at least not at first. I wasn't reading to gain some deep intellectual understanding of the world. I was reading because I wanted to build the habit, to strengthen something inside of me that had been weak for too long. I was reading the way someone starts running—slow, unsteady, struggling to catch their breath, but pushing through anyway, trusting that eventually, it would get easier.

And it did. But not in the way I expected.

It unlocked things inside me that I didn't even know were there. It made me realize that there were so many parts of myself—my emotions, my beliefs, even my sense of time—that had never been exercised like this. I had always thought of personal growth as something that happened on its own, something that came with age or experience. But reading showed me that growth could be—and in fact, sometimes had to be—intentional. It had to be worked on, every single day.

When you're young, you don't think about working out. Your body just works. You run without getting tired. You eat junk food without feeling the consequences. You drink however much you want and don't get hungover. But then, one day, things begin to change. You get winded going up the stairs. You don't recover from injuries as quickly. You drink the wrong kind of box wine and can't function right for a week. You realize your body isn't invincible, and if you want to keep it strong, you must put in the effort.

The same thing happens with your mind. When you're a kid, you don't think about exercising your thoughts, your emotions, your beliefs. They just *are.* But then, life happens. Stress piles up. Anxiety creeps in. Old ways of thinking don't work anymore. And if you haven't been training your mind—if you haven't been reading, reflecting, questioning—then suddenly, you're out of shape in a way that's much harder to fix.

Reading those hundred books made me realize that every part of life needs maintenance. My emotions needed to be exercised. My ability to handle stress needed to be worked on. My perspective on relationships, on time, on purpose—it all needed training. I wasn't only out of shape in my reading. I was out of shape in *life.*

And every book I picked up was another workout, another step toward strengthening the parts of me that had been neglected for too long.

And then there was the biggest lesson of all: time.

The more I read, the more I understood that time is finite. That every moment we spend avoiding growth, and avoiding hard things, is a moment we don't get back.

No one had ever told me that I needed to exercise my understanding of *the end.* No one had ever said, "Hey, you should sit with the fact that life isn't infinite, that you won't always have time to change, to fix things, to become who you want to be." But books taught me that. They made me confront things I had never thought about before. They made me realize that if I wasn't careful, I could end up like so many people I had seen—bitter, lost in their own thoughts, trapped by belief systems they had never questioned, never fought back against.

Just like an out-of-shape body catches up with you, so does an untrained mind. And I didn't want to reach the end of my one and only life only to realize that I had never put in the work to shape my thoughts, my emotions, and my ability to handle whatever came next.

So, reading became a necessity, as much as anything else I did to survive and thrive. A way to prepare myself for a future I had never truly considered before.

The Giving Tree, a picture book about a boy and the tree who loves him until the very end, was the first book I read that year. Like I said, I didn't get it at first. I read through it, and it didn't click. It wasn't that I didn't understand the words—it was that I didn't understand what the book was trying to tell me. I put it down, but

I found myself picking it up again later. And then again. Over the course of that year, I must have read parts of it ten times before it finally hit me.

By the end of the year, I realized that *The Giving Tree* was a lesson. A reflection of life itself. The way we take and take, the way we keep moving forward without ever stopping to consider what we're leaving behind. The way we don't practice for the end, or prepare for the fact that one day, we might look back and wonder: If we had done things differently, would we still end up alone?

That book made me think about my own life. It made me look at the people around me and how much I had relied on them—how much I had taken without always thinking about how to give back. I had always needed more than the average person. More patience, more understanding, more help just to get through life. My partner, my family, my friends—they had been my trees, always offering, always giving, and I had taken without thinking about whether I was leaving enough behind to sustain them.

One of the main reasons my life has changed so drastically over the past few years is because I am now acknowledging those things. I realized that I couldn't have it all. I couldn't keep taking and expect that the well would never run dry. There would come a time when I would have to make hard choices, choices that wouldn't always be easy but that would be necessary for my growth and for the well-being of the people who loved me.

The Giving Tree showed me that. The boy in the story never stopped to think about what the tree needed—only what he needed. And I had been doing the same thing. I had taken and taken, expecting the people in my life to always be there, always be willing to give. But life doesn't work that way. At some point, the tree becomes a stump.

And if you don't recognize that before it's too late, you'll end up sitting on it, wondering where the time went and what you'll do now that you're all alone.

That book made me rethink the way I approached relationships. I realized that giving back is about more than saying thank-you or making grand gestures—I needed to make sustainable choices. It was about knowing when to take and when to let things replenish. It was about knowing that just because something is available to you doesn't mean you should take all of it. It was about balance.

And that's when I started looking at my own life differently. I realized that I had been afraid of stepping into my own independence. I had been afraid of failing, so I leaned on others to hold me up. But that wasn't fair to them. And it wasn't fair to me, either. If I wanted to grow, if I wanted to be more than someone who just took, I had to give back. I had to stand on my own.

That was one of the hardest lessons I had to learn. It meant stepping out of my comfort zone. It meant accepting that I couldn't always rely on people to pick up the slack for me. Taking responsibility for my own growth. What I had taken in the past, and what I was going to do moving forward.

That realization was terrifying. But it was also freeing. See, for the first time in my life, I wasn't just thinking about survival. Or about just getting by. I was thinking about what kind of person I wanted to be. And I knew I didn't want to end up sitting on the stump.

And so, I began making changes—taking steps toward independence, even when they felt uncomfortable. I thought about what I could give instead of what I needed. Seeing my journey as something bigger than me alone. Because the truth is, none of us makes it alone. But if we don't contribute to the people and the world around us, we don't leave anything behind, either.

And maybe that's what growth is. Becoming stronger for yourself and making sure that the people who helped you along the way aren't left empty in the process.

Fish in a Tree is another book that was crucial to my growth. It's about a girl named Ally who struggles with dyslexia and has been hiding her inability to read. Through the help of her new middle school teacher, Ally gains confidence. She comes together with some other kids who don't quite fit in, but despite their differences, they build a sense of belonging. That resonated with me, because in a way, when I came forward with my story, I was putting out a call. I was reaching out—not only for myself, but for others like me. The ones who had slipped through the cracks. Those who had struggled, who felt left behind, who thought they were alone.

Not being able to read was one way I had defined myself, but it wasn't the only thing. There were so many parts of me—my Blackness, my ADHD, my PTSD, my OCD, where I was from, who raised me—that shaped my experience in ways I didn't always understand. And when I started speaking about my struggles, people like me came forward. People who had been carrying their own hidden battles. People who had felt left out, underestimated, forgotten. We came together and built a community. We lifted each other up.

And I am so, so grateful for that.

From the people who followed me from day one to the ones who recently found me, from the countless messages of support to the ones that shook me—"I can't read either," "I thought I was the only one," "I've been hiding this my whole life"—I saw that I wasn't alone. And neither were they. Learning to read helped me find my people.

But let me be real: The journey wasn't always fun. It still isn't. There were times when I felt like my life was worse than before. I was broke, anxious, and more aware of my own struggles than ever. Because when you start making changes, you can't ignore the things you used to look away from. It gets uncomfortable and forces you to see yourself in ways you might not want to. But that's part of the process. Change isn't always fun, but that doesn't mean it's not worth it.

Reading a hundred books in a year was hard. But you know what's even harder? Waking up every day and showing up. Pushing forward. Committing to something even when it feels impossible. The real challenge isn't just learning to read—it's refusing to give up. Because the only way to learn how to read is to read. The only way to move forward is to keep going.

You just have to do it.

16

READING IS MAGIC

The Power of Now: A Guide to Spiritual Enlightenment (1999), by Eckhart Tolle

I'm still new to it all. I can't sit here and say I'm an expert on manifestation, meditation, mindfulness, or almost anything else we're talking about in this book. But I can tell you what those things mean to me and how they've started to change my life. I'd like to think a book about someone who's in the process, and who it's working for, can also have a lot of value.

So many people talk about these concepts like they have them all figured out, like they've reached some higher state of knowing that the rest of us are struggling to understand. But I don't think that's how it works. I think we're all in different stages of figuring it out, and it's okay.

For me, meditation is something I do as much as I can. I don't always know if I'm doing it right. Sometimes I sit in silence and try to clear my mind, only to find it racing in a million different directions. Other times, I close my eyes, breathe deep, and feel myself slipping into something that almost makes sense—like I'm on the edge of some deeper understanding but not quite there yet. And then there are times when I just fall asleep. I've learned this is all part of the process. You don't have to shut everything off. You have to learn how to sit with it. Learning how to be comfortable with the thoughts and emotions that come up.

People think of manifestation as simply thinking about something enough times until it magically happens. That's not completely it. It's more like training yourself to see the possibilities. The opportunities. To create a reality where you actually believe in the things you're working toward. For a long time, I didn't believe in anything bigger than what I had in front of me. I never thought I could do something like learn to read or write a book. These things seemed impossible.

Meditation taught me to slow down enough to recognize my own patterns, my own ways of talking myself out of things before I'd even tried them. It made me aware of the constant dialogue in my head, the one that had been running my whole life without me even realizing it. I asked myself—what if I changed the conversation? What if, instead of telling myself all the reasons something wouldn't work, I began imagining what would happen if it did?

Manifestation sounds like wishful thinking. But it's more than that—it's about belief. It's about showing up every day and training your brain to see a different possibility than the one you were given. I had to break down years—decades—of conditioning that told me I wasn't someone who could achieve big things. That I wasn't someone who could be educated, who could be a teacher to others, who could even be the kind of person people looked up to. I saw how these same thought processes had shaped my entire life. And when you've never believed something about yourself, it takes time to change that belief.

But I learned that's the first step. You have to believe it *before* you see it. And meditation helped me sit with myself long enough to begin rewriting my own narrative. When I first tried meditation, it wasn't easy. It wasn't like I sat down one day, closed my eyes, and suddenly had a whole new outlook on life. No, it was frustrating. It was messy. Some days, I was so impatient I'd give up after a few minutes. But I kept coming back to it. Kept practicing. And slowly, I was seeing how my mind worked. I began to notice my own habits—the way I'd talk myself out of good things before they could even happen. The way I'd assume failure before I even tried. Then, magically, failure came.

If you don't believe something is possible for you, you're never going to work toward it. You won't even let yourself try. And if you don't try, I'm sorry to tell you, it won't happen. It becomes a self-fulfilling prophecy. I had to break the cycle. I had to start believing in things I couldn't see yet. Because belief is what makes you take the first step. It's what keeps you going when things get hard. It's what makes you put in the work even when there's no guarantee of success.

I had spent most of my life believing only in what was right in front of me. And what was in front of me was struggle. Limitation. The idea that people like me didn't do big things. But once I changed the way I thought, I began seeing the world differently. I saw doors where before, I had only seen walls. And it wasn't because those doors suddenly appeared out of nowhere. They had always been there. I just hadn't been able to see them before.

Meditation and manifestation haven't instantly fixed my life or removed all the obstacles in my path. But they've helped me see the possibilities. They've helped me change my relationship with struggle. Instead of seeing struggle as proof that I'm stuck, I've begun to see it as part of the process. Part of the journey. And the more I embrace this, the more I realize the only real limitations are the ones I put on myself.

So now, when I sit down to meditate, I don't pressure myself to have some grand revelation. I let myself feel what I feel. I let myself imagine the kind of life I want to create, and then I take that feeling with me into the real world. I act on it. I make decisions based on it. And little by little, my reality shifts.

Because here's the thing about manifestation—it's *not* magic. It's action. It's about setting your sights on something bigger than yourself and then doing the work to get there. And for me, the work starts with believing it's even possible in the first place.

One of the things I always say when I talk to people about mindset is this: If you're in hell, you might as well learn how to decorate. That might sound weird but hear me out. If you're dealing with anxiety, depression, self-doubt—whatever it is—you can sit in it and let it consume you, or you can try to make it a little more livable. If your mind is already a tough place to be, why not try to find ways to make it better? Maybe it won't ever fully go away, maybe you'll always have those struggles, but it doesn't mean you can't find moments of peace inside of them.

For me, this has been the biggest realization. You must work on yourself the way you work on anything else. You must believe yourself. You have to say, *It's happening, the wheels are in motion for what I want, what do I do to keep going?* If you stop working on your mind, your thoughts get weak. They spiral. They turn against you. You start believing the worst things about yourself.

Saying something won't happen and living like that's your expectation? Well, guess what? It's not going to happen. Why wouldn't it work the other way around?

So, I try to be intentional about the way I think. I don't just wake up and hope for a good day. I try to create one. I try to set the tone for how I want my mind to function. This is where meditation helps.

It's a reset button. A moment to stop and just *be*. On days where my brain won't shut up, where I sit there frustrated because I can't stop thinking about my problems—even on those days, I try.

And manifestation? It's planting the seeds. Creating the reality in your mind before you ever see it in front of you. I don't simply say, *I want to be successful*, and hope it happens. I act like someone who is on the path to success. I think about the version of me who has already made it, and I ask myself, *What would he be doing right now?* Would he be sitting around, doubting himself? Or would he be putting in the work, every single day, even when it feels impossible?

That's what I mean when I say I manifest things. I act as if they're already happening. And over time, it changes the way I see myself. It changes what I believe I'm capable of. It makes the impossible feel possible. It makes things feel real before they actually are. It changes the way I look at the world—and allows me to see real, tangible paths that I wouldn't be able to if I weren't looking. And that's a powerful thing.

So, when I think about meditation, and about manifestation, I don't think of them as these separate ideas. To me, they go hand in hand. One is about clearing the noise. The other is about focusing on the vision. And when you put them together, you feel like maybe you can create the life you want.

One of the biggest realizations I had when I started reading *The Power of Now* was how much of my life I had spent outside of the present moment. It was almost like I had never truly been *here*. My mind was always somewhere else, in another time, another place, tangled up in thoughts that had nothing to do with what was right in front of me. It was like I had been living on autopilot, trapped between two places: the past, where regrets and mistakes lived, and the future, where worries and fears waited for me.

I wasn't in the present. I was in some dark reflection of the present that had no awareness of the *now* and could only look forward and back—never at where your feet were planted. The future was a place of fears, not options. And the past was a place of regret, not lessons.

I thought about all the times I had replayed conversations in my head, thinking about what I *should* have said or done. I thought about the nights I'd lain awake, thinking about where I had gone wrong, how I had messed up, how I could have done things differently. And just as often, I was stuck worrying about things that hadn't even happened yet—stressing over the future, over money, over where I was going to be in five years, over whether I'd ever make it. It was like my brain was constantly running, but I was never actually *present* for my own life.

And once I began paying attention to this cycle of constant worry and self-doubt, I realized how much it was holding me back.

That's what manifestation and mindfulness are all about. Awareness. Recognizing where your thoughts are leading you, where your energy is going, and whether or not a certain direction is serving you. Because if all your energy is caught up in the past or tied up in a future that hasn't happened yet, then you're not *living*. You're merely existing in the present's dark reflection; the space between what was and what could be, never fully embracing *what is*.

For a long time, my energy was always directed toward survival. It was all I knew. I wasn't thinking about building anything, creating anything, or even dreaming of a different life. I was just trying to get through the day. When you spend years scraping by, getting through each moment the best you can—you begin to think that's *all* life is. You believe that's all life *can* be.

As I learned about mindfulness, I saw that my thoughts had been shaping my reality this entire time. I just wasn't the one who'd chosen which thoughts to start with.

If I spent all day focusing on how I wasn't good enough, how I was never going to get anywhere, then I was making that my truth. I was reinforcing it every day, repeating those beliefs in my head until they became the foundation of how I saw myself. And when that's the foundation you build your life on, there's nowhere to go but down.

It wasn't until I began thinking differently—truly allowing myself to believe change was possible—that I saw things were shifting. It wasn't easy, and it didn't happen overnight, but little by little, I began redirecting my thoughts. Instead of waking up and immediately thinking about what was wrong in my life, I tried to focus on *what was right*. Instead of telling myself all the reasons why something wouldn't work, I asked myself, *What if it does?* What if things go *right* for once? What if I *am* capable of more than I thought? What if I can break out of the cycle I've been in my whole life?

At first, it felt like I was lying to myself. It felt fake, like I was saying things that weren't true. But I realized something: I had been lying to myself for years already—telling myself I *couldn't* do things, I wasn't smart enough, I would never succeed. If I could believe *those* things, why couldn't I believe something different? Those things weren't reality either. Why couldn't I transfer that same energy into believing in *possibilities* instead of *limitations*?

And then, everything slowly changed. Not all at once, not in some big dramatic way, but in small, steady steps. And the more I practiced it, the more I *saw* the change happening around me.

Opportunities I never noticed before began to appear. People showed up in my life who genuinely wanted to help. I was reading, and learning, and for the first time, I saw a future that wasn't just about *getting by*—it was about actually *living*.

And it all sprang from changing my mindset. Choosing to live *now*, in this moment, instead of being trapped in the past or consumed by the future. Deciding to set the foundation for something different, to believe in something better—even when I wasn't sure I deserved it. And then to *step into opportunity* when it comes.

And the more I do it, the more I realize—it works.

The process was slow. I had to catch myself over and over, stopping negative thoughts before they took root. I had to remind myself constantly that I was capable, I was learning, I was changing. And that's what *The Power of Now* showed me: I was always caught in these loops of thought, these old patterns, and I had to make a choice—either keep living in them or step outside of them.

I learned that meditation is *noticing* your thoughts instead of getting caught up in them. Sitting with yourself without judgment, letting those thoughts pass by without chasing them down. And this was *hard* for me. My mind has always been loud. I've always had thoughts racing at a hundred miles an hour, always replaying conversations, thinking about the past, dreading the future. But when I tried to *observe* my thoughts instead of getting caught up in them, I saw that *I* wasn't my thoughts. I was something *behind* them, something deeper.

This was a huge revelation. If I wasn't my thoughts, then I had the power to change them.

For me, this meant doing things that felt unnatural at first: Telling myself I could learn to read, even when I felt like I never would. Picturing myself as an author, as someone who could write a book, even before I had written a single page. Believing I could change my entire life, even when my circumstances didn't reflect that yet. And eventually, things fell into place—because I was *acting* like they were possible.

Whether you believe in manifestation or not, your thoughts shape your reality every single day. If you go through life expecting failure, then you'll probably find it. But if you tell yourself a different story—if you see yourself as someone who *can* succeed, someone who *deserves* happiness, someone who *is* capable—then you move in that direction, even if you don't realize it at first.

This is what meditation has helped me with the most. It's given me the space to slow down and recognize those thoughts as they come up. It's allowed me to separate *who I am* from *what I think.*

I still have bad days. I still catch myself falling back into old patterns. But now, I notice when it's happening. And that awareness is everything. It is what allows me to shift, to redirect, to step back and remind myself of what I'm working toward.

Because at the end of the day, manifestation is about becoming the kind of person who can *create* what you want. It's about believing in yourself enough to take the steps, to do the work, to trust the process even when you can't see the results yet. And that's something I'll always be learning, always be working on.

Because the more I practice it, the more I see just how much is possible.

17

READING IS NOW

Percy Jackson and the Olympians: The Lightning Thief (2005),
by Rick Riordan

EVEN NOW, AFTER ALL THIS TIME, after all this growth, I still struggle. Learning to read didn't erase the difficulties of my life—it just changed them. It gave me more tools, more options, but the world keeps moving, responsibilities don't wait for me to catch up, and I still face daily challenges that other people take for granted.

It's something I wrestle with all the time—being a partner and a father who can't navigate life the way most people can. Simple things, like booking a hotel or a flight, are still a struggle. I can't go to a parent-teacher meeting and review my child's assignments the way other parents can. Properly signing documents, setting up insurance, booking appointments—tasks that most people barely think about still feel like mountains to me. I rely on my partner, Anne, for things I wish I could handle on my own. I don't want her to have to teach me. I don't want her to have to manage my life on top of her own. It's not fair to her. And yet, there are things I simply can't do alone—not yet.

I'm trying. Every day, I'm trying. But I have to build something inside myself that wasn't there before. And that takes time. Forever, maybe.

But time doesn't slow down for me. Bills still need to be paid. My kids still need to be taken care of. Forms still need to be signed, schedules still need to be kept. It is the reality of my life, and it's one I must accept while I work toward changing it.

Much of why I even tried to learn how to read was so I could learn how to give more than I take. And that's still what I want. But wanting it and being able to do it—those are two very different things. The reality is, I've spent so much of my life in survival mode, trying to keep my head above water, that sometimes I struggle to remember what it means to be fully present in a relationship. When you're always in a state of trying to catch up, it's easy to miss the little things. The gestures, the conversations, the moments that show someone you truly care. And because I've spent so long without the ability to fully engage, I've had to work twice as hard to make up for it.

There are times when I get so wrapped up in getting through the day that I forget to do the things that matter most—expressing gratitude, making the other person feel special, showing love in ways beyond just words. I don't mean to. But between struggling to keep up with everyday tasks, the weight of feeling left behind, and the frustration of not being able to do things as easily as others, I sometimes shut down instead of leaning in. I avoid conversations that feel complicated. I pull away when I should be drawing closer. And none of that is fair to the people I love.

When my life took off after TikTok, suddenly, for the first time, I had some level of financial freedom. I could pay off household expenses, buy things for people, take care of things that I never could before. And it felt like this massive step toward independence—like finally, I was able to contribute more than I had in the past. But money doesn't solve everything. There's still all the stuff in between. The conversations, the emotional labor, the responsibilities that go beyond just providing.

The hardest part of all is realizing the ways I've hurt people. Not because I meant to, or because I wanted to, but because I didn't know how not to. For a long time, I was someone who lied, cheated, stole—sometimes because those things made me feel like I had some kind of control over my life, but often because I couldn't see any other way. Sometimes when I was hurt, I found ways to get even, even if the other person didn't deserve it. I didn't see it for what it was at the time, but looking back, I know now that a lot of my worst behaviors came from fear. Fear of being abandoned. Of being seen as weak. Fear of being hurt first. And in trying to protect myself, I ended up hurting people who didn't deserve it.

And yeah, people hurt me too. Most of the time, they didn't mean to. Sometimes, it was because I didn't tell them what I needed, and other times, it was because they had things I didn't, and that alone felt like a reminder of everything I lacked.

Watching people go through the world with ease—reading menus and online articles, sending emails and texts—felt like a slap in the face every time. It made me feel small, incapable, and like I would never catch up. And instead of admitting my insecurity, I lashed out in other ways. I built walls. I created distance. I sabotaged things before they had a chance to fall apart on their own.

Maybe I thought telling people the truth about my illiteracy and everything else would fix things. Like the moment they knew, everything would fall into place. But that's not how it works. Telling the truth was only the first step, not the solution. People knew where I was coming from, but it didn't erase the years of pain, the damage I had done, or the work that still needed to be done. And the truth is, not everyone is meant to make it to the finish line with me. Some people are only meant to be part of the journey, and that's okay.

My partner is not responsible for me. No one else is. It's no one's job to teach me how to be a man, or a good partner. That's on me. And if I don't get it right, that's also on me. I have to be the one who takes accountability and puts in the effort.

I'm trying. Every day, I'm trying. To be better, to show up more, to communicate, to be present. It's not easy, and I still have a long way to go. But I refuse to be the person I used to be. I refuse to let my struggles define me. And no matter how hard it gets, I refuse to give up on the people who matter most.

There's so much chatter about not playing the victim, about not blaming others and being strong. And I think recently people have been looking at their inner child and asking the hard questions: *But what if someone did fail him? What if someone should have done more for her? What if they got hurt, and someone else did it to them?*

We are always told that personal responsibility is key, that we should take ownership of our actions, that our choices define us. And yes, in many ways, this is all true. But what happens when the choices that shaped us weren't even our own? What happens when our earliest memories of the world are of people who should have protected us *choosing* not to? What happens when the foundation we were given to stand on was cracked from the beginning?

I have a role in every part of my life, including when I have been failed by others. But it doesn't mean I have to take it all on, to carry it all as if it were mine to bear. There is a difference between owning your part and taking responsibility for things that were never yours to start. That's the piece I struggled with for most of my life.

I was the kind of person who would always look inward first, always assume I was the problem. If something went wrong, I'd immediately wonder: *What did I do?* If someone left, I'd think: *How did I drive them away?* If I struggled, I'd blame myself: *Why can't I be better? Smarter? Stronger?* It was a constant cycle of self-blame, a never-ending loop of believing that if I was just a little more *something*—capable, disciplined, put-together—then maybe I wouldn't have had to struggle so much.

But the truth is *I wasn't the problem.* Who I was, who I am, was not and is not the problem.

It took me a long time to realize this. A long time to even allow myself to *think* it. Because admitting it means acknowledging that I was let down. I was abandoned in certain ways, left to figure things out alone when I should have had help. And that is a painful thing to confront.

It's painful because it makes you grieve for the person you were. The child who didn't know any better. The teenager who acted out because he didn't have the words to say, *I need help*. The young man who kept making the same mistakes because he was never taught another way. You grieve for all the versions of yourself that carried the weight of something that wasn't yours to hold in the first place.

And it took me such a long time to be honest with myself and accept all this. Because I'm not some outside observer, am I? I'm the one who lived that shit. I'm the living consequence of the things that happened to me. I wasn't equipped to equip myself.

That's the thing people don't always understand about healing. Healing is about *reckoning*—standing in front of everything you've been through and allowing yourself to feel the weight of it without letting it consume you.

Because, yeah, people failed me. I didn't get what I needed in certain areas. And if I refuse to acknowledge that, I'll keep carrying those failures as if they are my own. I'll keep believing that every hardship was something I should have been strong enough to handle, rather than recognizing that some of those hardships should never have been mine to bear in the first place.

The world tells us that the moment we point a finger at someone else, we're making excuses. If we acknowledge the ways we were failed, we're choosing to be victims. But that's bullshit. Because recognizing where we weren't given what we needed isn't about *staying* in that place but understanding it so we can finally move forward.

And that's what I'm doing now. I'm learning to separate what *is* my responsibility from what was never mine to begin with. I'm learning that I can own my story without making myself the villain in it. And I'm learning that strength means refusing to let that hurt define me forever. For so long, I kept parts of myself locked away because it was easier. I could tell bits and pieces of my story, enough to satisfy curiosity without really letting anyone in. Especially in relationships—girlfriends would get fragments, the outlines of what I had been through, but never the full picture. I told myself it was to protect them, but I was actually protecting myself. Because if they knew everything, would they still want to be with me? Would they still see me the same way? Or would they look at me with pity, hesitation, and doubt?

Anne was the first person to truly know me. The first person I trusted enough to lay it all out, to show her the parts of myself I had always kept hidden. And it changed everything. For the first time, I wasn't merely coasting through surface-level relationships. I was seen. I was understood. But even that wasn't enough, because now that someone finally knew me, the next question was—did they still love me? Did they still want me? It's one thing to be known, it's another thing to be accepted.

And there it is—not everyone who knows your story will know how to love you. It takes more than understanding. It takes patience, effort, a willingness to meet you where you are. This applies to the people in my life, but it also applies to me. I have to be the one to love myself first. I have to be the one to meet myself where I am, to have patience with myself, to equip myself with the tools I need to keep growing. And man, I'm trying.

For so much of my life, I hadn't truly met myself. I hadn't looked at my life, my struggles, my failures, and taken them in for what they were. I didn't listen to my own pain, I didn't acknowledge what I had been through, I didn't even question why I was the way I was. I kept going, kept surviving, without ever stopping to process any of it.

Even though I've spent years wanting to blame myself, I've had to learn to let it go. I was a kid. I didn't know any better. Like I said, I wasn't equipped to equip myself. That was supposed to be someone else's job. That's what I keep trying to remind myself of when those old voices creep in, the ones that say, "You should have tried harder, you should have known better." Because no—I was a child. I did the best I could with what I had. And if no one gave me the right tools back then, that wasn't on me.

This realization is what made my TikTok community so important to me. They became my people. My safe space. The place where I could be fully myself, flaws and all. If I'm feeling alone, if I'm struggling, if I'm tempted to slip back into old habits—because yeah, I still have those moments—I go Live. And suddenly I'm not alone. I'm talking to people who understand, who see me, who support me. We're reading together, sharing stories, crying, laughing, feeling everything in real time. And the best part? I have to read to keep that connection going. I have to be able to understand the comments, to respond, to engage. So, every single day, I'm reinforcing the very skill that once made me feel so disconnected from the world.

And they get it. My community, my people—they get it. They don't rush me, or judge me, or get frustrated if I miss something and get it wrong. They help me. They repeat comments if I miss them. They work with me. And over time I'm even recognizing familiar names, remembering people who come back time and time again. It's like having an entire room full of friends who show up just to be with me. What an incredible gift. I'm so lucky.

It feels like unconditional love. And I think that's all I've ever wanted. It's probably what everyone wants. To be seen, to be known, and to be loved anyway. The only difference is, I have a built-in test for it. Because before anyone can fully be in my life, before I can even think about having a relationship, I must know that love exists without conditions. Because if someone can't accept me fully, then they were never truly there for me in the first place. All those folks on social media? They follow me *because* of my shortcomings.

How cool is that?

Where I am now, and where I'm going, is a complicated thing to talk about. Because the truth is, I don't always know. Life is still shifting under my feet, and I'm still figuring out how to keep my balance. But I do know this: I've come a long way, and I'm not done yet.

Now I can see how much I was taking from the people around me—how much I relied on them to fill in the gaps, to help me navigate a world I wasn't equipped to handle on my own.

It's a tough thing to admit. Because I never wanted to be a burden. I never wanted anyone to feel like they had to carry me. Even though sometimes I wanted to *feel* that kind of backup. I'd even ask for it, from people who had already gone far above and beyond for me and didn't owe me one more thing. I'd ask them to catch me anyway.

For a long time, they did. And that wasn't fair to them. It wasn't fair to Anne. It wasn't fair to my kids. It wasn't fair to the people who cared about me so much they sacrificed themselves to be there for me.

In the end, it wasn't even fair to me. I was cheating myself out of necessary growth. The more I relied on others, the more I convinced myself I wasn't capable. I'd look how they handled things and think I could never be like them. So I thought I couldn't do things on my own, rather than realizing my way might just be a little different. No, I couldn't talk to people like Anne did; I couldn't read the teacher's note and then be ready to converse in a parent-teacher conference with her confidence.

I wasn't stupid and never had been, so I had to stop acting like I was.

These days I don't even want to be saved. I want to stand on my own, whatever that means for me, no matter what the results. And I want to be the kind of person who can give back, who can lift others up instead of always needing a hand.

That's what this whole book is about. Trying, so hard, to give back.

That's why I've pushed myself to keep going, to keep learning, to keep growing. Like I said, it's why I wanted to read. It's definitely part of the reason I've written this book, to share the truth and the hope. It's why I get on TikTok and try to show the world what's possible for someone who was written off as a hopeless stereotype for decades.

It's not like I have it all figured out now. I'm not trying for one second to make anyone think I'm saying I've got all my shit together and this is a manual for you to do the exact same thing.

If anything, I hope you're getting the opposite message: There's no such thing as being finished learning. There's no such thing as completing self-improvement and not needing any more.

There's no such thing as perfection.

Imagine how boring it would be if there were. Nothing more to think about or learn or try to do. Being good at everything and never needing instructions would be horrible. We humans need challenges, both physical and mental.

No matter how far I've come, there are still moments where I feel like I'm falling behind. It's hard not to get super critical of myself sometimes because of it. I'm not even close to where I'd like to be in the learning game.

I have to remind myself all the time: I am not where I used to be.

And that's enough.

There's another important part of this too. The emotional side of things. Reading wasn't the only thing I had to learn. After growing up thinking I had to *be a man* and *man up*, it's been a real challenge to admit my weaknesses, fears, and sometimes even love. It was my impression that "real men" were supposed to be "too cool" to have feelings. This turned out to be false, of course. How could anyone admire a guy who stays trapped in his own ignorance on purpose? He doesn't look cool; he looks like a fool.

I had to learn how to communicate about *everything*. How to be present and honest in a relationship. More than honest, I needed to be *involved*. Thinking people can't spend their whole lives just reacting to what everyone else says, I needed to contribute to the relationship. I needed to show love instead of assuming people knew I cared.

That's something I'm still working on too. I spent so much of my life keeping people at arm's length, giving them only enough to stick around but never enough to truly know me. And now, I'm undoing all of that. I'm letting people in. Being honest. Learning how to have the conversations I used to avoid.

It's not easy. Sometimes I still fall into old patterns. I still get quiet when I should speak up. Or shut down when things feel overwhelming. But I catch myself now. And I try to do better.

It's wild to think about how much has changed so fast. A few years ago, I was struggling in silence, carrying the weight of all this shame and fear, feeling like I was the only person in the world who had to deal with this. Now, I have thousands of people who remind me every day that I'm not alone. People who don't even know me but who celebrate my wins with me. They help me see that I have something worth sharing.

And that's the biggest thing I've learned: I'm not alone. None of us are.

So, where am I going from here?

I don't have all the answers. But I know what I want. I want to keep learning. I want to keep growing. I want to keep pushing myself to do things I never thought I could do. I want to be a better father, a better partner, a better friend. I want to continue telling my story, not only because it helps me, but because I know it helps other people too.

I want to show people that it's never too late. No matter where your starting point is, you can always go farther. That version of yourself you dream about? The one who's confident, capable, and free? That person is already inside you. You just have to do the work to bring them to the surface.

* * *

The book that represents the theme of this chapter is *The Lightning Thief* from the Percy Jackson series. It was another book that came highly recommended, and my family and I ended up reading it together. My partner, my stepson, and I took turns reading chapters. It wasn't always easy—the names of Greek gods and some of the terms were hard for me—but we did it together. And that meant something.

What stuck with me about Percy's story was that he spent his whole childhood not knowing he was different. Not knowing he was a half-blood, that he was half-human, half-god. Then, suddenly, at age eleven or twelve, he was thrown into a world that he didn't even know existed. A world where so many of the kids around him already knew who they were. They had spent their whole lives understanding the gods, their powers, their history. Percy had to learn it all from scratch. And the wildest part? While he was still learning, he had to act like he already knew. He had to pretend to get it, to fake confidence while figuring it all out on the fly.

That's exactly how I felt when my story started gaining attention. Suddenly, I wasn't just some guy learning to read—I was on social media, on mainstream news, on the radio, on TV. People were asking me to come speak to students and teachers. I was thrown into a world I hadn't been prepared for, full of people who already knew how things worked. I'd get asked for things I didn't understand, like "Can we get a headshot and a short bio?" What was a short bio? Who was supposed to write it? There were reading terms I hadn't learned yet, like "TBR list," and logistics for public speaking that I had never even considered. Like Percy, I had to fake it. The only difference this time? I finally had the resources to learn.

Fake it till you make it isn't just a saying. It's real. And it works. But the key is that whatever you're faking, it must align with your goals and values. Show up, even when you don't feel ready. Even when you feel like you don't belong.

So go out and fail. That's right. Fail! Fail a couple of times. Get rejected, get corrected, get back up. Because every single time you put yourself in an uncomfortable position and try? It's a win. That's the real goal. To try. To exercise who you want to be. To step into new situations, knowing you don't have all the answers but trusting yourself to figure them out.

For me, I never would have believed I'd be here now, an author, giving speeches, traveling, learning more and more every day. But I showed up. I kept trying. I took every moment I felt lost or out of place as a chance to grow. And now? Now, I know that's the only way you ever really succeed. By doing it scared. By failing forward. By learning as you go.

Because here's the truth: As long as you're trying, you're *not* failing.

18

READING IS FOR INNER CHILDREN

Llama Llama Red Pajama (2015), by Anna Dewdney

When I began writing this book and thinking about the books that most inspired me in my reading journey and which of those books would be featured in each chapter, my editor asked if we could include a few more adult titles in my list than I originally had. I get it—most people reading this book will be adults who probably read kids' books a long time ago, and what value do children's books have for an adult?

Well, a lot, in my opinion.

At first, when I was in the very early stages of learning, I wasn't thinking about what kind of books I was supposed to read. I was just trying to read, period. All my life I'd heard people talk about this great mystery book they couldn't guess the ending to, or some thriller that kept them up at night, or even the whole *Twilight* and *Fifty Shades of Grey* stuff everyone was raving about. I was behind on *all* of that.

Naturally, when I first decided to learn to read, I thought it would be easy, and I'd be right up to speed with all the bestsellers.

You know what? When you can't read, those regular paperback books look like a wall of black ink when you open them up. It's overwhelming.

I figured out pretty quick that I was going to have to approach it the way most people do when they're children: I was going to have to try children's books first. In fact, when I went to the bookstore, the books I was looking for were *picture books—beginner books* for children.

Here's the thing, though: Kids are a tough audience. You may think they aren't, but think about it, the loudest kids are the bored ones. If you want to keep their attention, you've got to work for it.

Even with picture books.

A grown man reading *Llama Llama Red Pajama* and even *struggling* with it? Some people might think this is a little embarrassing for me to admit. It's not something you see every day, I know.

But I don't see it that way. Finishing a book—any book—was an accomplishment. It built my confidence, and confidence is half the battle when you're trying to learn something new.

One of the biggest reasons people who struggle with reading don't want to read is because they don't feel like they're making progress. They read the first few pages of a book, but they never finish it because every single page feels like it takes forever to get through. If you're opening *War and Peace* with the idea of working through every word, I can almost guarantee that by the time you get to the bottom of the first page, you will have forgotten what happened at the top, especially if it takes you a long time.

But like I've stressed several times now, you also wouldn't decide to run three miles after years on the sofa watching reruns with a full-on marathon. You'd collapse immediately. On top of that, you probably wouldn't be super motivated to try running a marathon again. Or even a few yards.

This is what that wall of black text feels like to someone who can't read. It looks impossible, so why bother? It would be a hundred times easier to just give up and return to life the way it was . . . but the first time you can't fill out an insurance form in the emergency room when your kid has had a fall, you'll remember how much harder the inability to read is. It's worth *any* amount of work to overcome.

I'm here to tell you from experience the easiest way to approach learning to read. And that's with picture books. When you're learning anything new, you don't go straight to the hardest version. You build up to it. If you're learning a new language, you learn basic words, not advanced literature. If you're learning to lift weights, you don't load the bar with three hundred pounds. And with reading, it's the same. I'm not a marathon guy, so children's books were my way of lifting five-pound weights before moving up to something heavier.

There were some surprising bonuses. A big one was that reading children's books let me experience something I hadn't felt much before: the satisfaction of completion. A story that I'd *read.* A *lot* of things are hard to complete when you can't read or write—remember that insurance form we talked about a minute ago? That's only one!

So, I set out to read a book, I got through it, and I finished it. I could set it aside and take on another one, then add it to the finished pile. I swear that feeling of finishing something, of actually crossing that line, was *powerful.* It made me want to keep going.

Exactly the way a new runner might feel after running half a block every day for a week and feeling exhausted by it, then finding the next day they can do the whole block. And on it goes from there.

At the same time, reading children's books as an adult is a completely different experience emotionally than I expected. For me, it wasn't just about learning to read, though that was the main thing—it was about realizing what I had missed all those years ago.

There's a kind of nostalgia people have when they think about the books they read as kids. They remember their parent reading to them before bed, they remember their favorite characters, the stories that stuck with them. The early moments when their imagination started to soar, when they began to make up things that weren't real, but which fulfilled them anyway. I never had that.

Since beginning my quest to read, I've spoken with many readers and writers, and you wouldn't believe how often they say their favorite book is something they read as a kid or young adult. Some of the YA books I read have been around for *decades* but to me they were brand new. *Harriet the Spy* was written in 1964. *Lord of the Flies* was released in 1954. One of my favorites, *The Outsiders*, was published in 1967 (the author, S. E. Hinton, was only sixteen when she wrote it; when I was sixteen, I couldn't even read the instructions on a shampoo bottle!).

You get the idea. Books weren't a part of my childhood. So when I read these books for the first time, it was like stepping into a part of childhood I had never experienced.

I think I'd go so far as to say reading those books gave me an idea of what life was expected to be. How people grow and develop; how their daily occupation changes with age; how homes change; and more than anything, how relationships change. Apart from my family, which even I knew wasn't "normal" in the usual accepted sense, I had *no* real clues as to how people developed and lived together.

Now I can talk to other people about these things.

That's one of the best things about books—they connect people. When I mention a specific book on TikTok, thousands of people comment about how it was their favorite growing up. People share memories about their parents reading to them, about how that book shaped them. And I was only discovering all this now. It made me feel like I was getting a late invitation to a party that had been going on for years.

I'm guessing some books hit differently as an adult, though, versus reading them as a kid.

Take *The Giving Tree* again—when I first read it, I didn't fully understand it. It was sad to me. I felt bad for the tree, and mad at the boy who turned into a man and used up the tree. Why was this a book so many people loved? Why was this the message the author wanted to tell children? It was a kids' book, and it made me sad.

I don't know whether kids have this same experience or not. Does a child reading *The Giving Tree* for the first time understand the symbolism in the book? Do they also wonder about the heart of the tree and the man? I don't know.

I do know that lots of kids read books in school, where they get to discuss the meanings and significance of every chapter as they go along, which I can see as being a healthy thing to do. Kind of like built-in therapy.

I wonder if I would have been a happier kid if I'd been able to read and take part in those classroom discussions. In the case of *The Giving Tree*, it took reading that book over and over for me to finally get the message about selfishness. And it's a great message. As a dad now, I can say I'd like my kids to learn that one while they're still young.

But there was another thing I hadn't counted on when I started my reading journey—rereading a book, sometimes even several times, to understand the message. It was a surprise to me how stories layer with rereading. Since I wasn't a strong reader, every time I read a book again, it was like reading it for the first time (only technically easier). I could see new things, understand new ideas. And that was another unexpected part of learning to read later in life—I was getting something out of books that I might not have appreciated as a kid.

But what about adults who already know how to read? Is there any value in going back and reading children's books? I think so. There's something about the simplicity of those stories that makes the messages clearer. The way they distill big ideas into something small and digestible—friendship, love, loss, perseverance. Those themes don't go away simply because we grow up. And sometimes, reading a children's book as an adult lets you see all of life in a new way.

If you've read *Charlie and the Chocolate Factory*, do you even open a bar of chocolate without half-looking for a golden ticket? Okay, maybe you do, but if you've read that book it's hard not to think about the magic of the unexpected in everyday things. Same with the Harry Potter books or any other book with fantasy or supernatural elements.

Holes will help you appreciate your freedom, and maybe to see those guys picking up trash on the side of the road in a different way.

Charlotte's Web sure instilled more respect for animals and spiders in me; it was part of my journey to veganism. But the funny thing is that giving personalities to those animals didn't just make me think, like, *maybe rats aren't so bad if they're like Templeton*, but that the animals represent characters we all know in real life. Using Templeton as an example, E. B. White shows how the sourest, nastiest disposition can be hiding a heart of gold—someone who would genuinely step up for you if you needed them. How you never know someone's story.

Reading these stories reminded me of the basics, of the simple truths we sometimes forget when life gets complicated. We all learned the golden rule—"treat others as you would like others to treat you"—as children; but it's not something we think much about as adults. Children's literature is such a great way to communicate important ideas and morals in easy, engaging terms that *anyone* can understand. Plus, it seems like lots of people out there have forgotten some of the basic human lessons that are taught to young readers. Wouldn't hurt to give them another look.

This idea of simplicity is also what makes children's books such a good tool for struggling readers; sometimes you recognize the parallel in a story and you want to read on to find out how to handle it in real life.

There's no line I know of that clearly marks where young reader books become young adult books: Honestly, I enjoyed them all, but eventually the themes get more sophisticated, and the imagery and symbolism become more subtle and complex. As an ongoing reader, working a little harder to get there is more satisfying, and I find that with books meant for slightly older readers, the messages become even more universal. As in, they're not only for adolescent kids.

Books like *Percy Jackson* or *The Chronicles of Narnia*—they don't seem like kids' books exactly; they maybe skew for younger readers, but they each have a compelling storytelling magic that pulls you in. And they help to build my confidence, both in my reading and in my navigation of the world around me—and as I help my kids find their way in this increasingly crazy world.

Every book I finish, I feel like I'm leveling up. Every single one I finish is an accomplishment. I tell myself, "If I can read a hundred young adult books, I can go to college." That's the goal right now.

Textbooks. Those will be the next challenge. And I'm building my way there, the same way I did when I set out on this journey—one step at a time.

Reading is everywhere. It's even in technology, which has been a huge part of this journey too. Technology that is pretty useless if you're illiterate.

For example, I use Google voice-to-text, I listen to audiobooks, I post on TikTok and respond to messages there. Some people look at technology like it's a bad thing, like it's making people lazier. But for me, it's been the opposite. It's been a bridge to *so many* new destinations. It's helped me get to places I wouldn't have been able to reach otherwise.

Audiobooks, especially, have been a game changer. Listening to books has helped me understand words, hear how things are pronounced (that's a huge benefit), and absorb information in a way that works for me. If I miss something, it's easy enough to go back and listen again. It's sort of like how it must have been for kids who had books read to them when they were young—they listened to parents and teachers reading, and that's how they learned.

I used to think audiobooks didn't count as reading. But this is another myth I had to unlearn. Reading is more than looking at words on a page. It's about understanding, picturing, imagining, learning, and engaging with a story or an idea. And audiobooks have given me access to books I might have otherwise struggled with.

When I listened to *Ishmael* (discussed in the next chapter), I thought about the way we define intelligence. This book makes you question what it means to be civilized, to be knowledgeable. And for a long time, I thought intelligence and reading were the same thing. That if you couldn't read, you weren't smart. But it's not true. I was always smart. I just didn't have the right tools. And now that I have them, I'm realizing how much I'm capable of.

So, when people ask me, "What's the best way to learn to read?" I tell them: start small, choose what feels doable. If a children's book is what gets you turning pages, then read a children's book. If listening to an audiobook helps you get through a story, then listen to an audiobook. If it's an unabridged audiobook, you can read along with the book and *see* the words while you hear them. That's huge. I know that's essentially how a lot of folks learn a foreign language—by following the closed captioning on the screen while listening to the voices of the actors.

The point is, if you need to take it slow, take it slow. Give yourself all the incentives you need to keep going, treat yourself to stories that thrill you or advice books that tell you how to do something you've been wanting to learn. There are countless options. The only thing that matters is that you keep going.

Reading is what you take from it. And for me, it's been about reclaiming something I never had. A connection to books, to stories, to a whole world I was missing out on. And now that I'm in it, I'm not stopping.

And you know what? Even if you're racing, you still have to begin where you are and go from there. No one's winning gold medals for not training.

One of the biggest lessons I've learned on this journey is that reading is about *connection*. Not just to other people (though as I said, that's a big one), but connection to the world around you. When I pick up a book, I'm reading a story, yes, but I'm also engaging with ideas, emotions, and perspectives that were previously out of my reach. And that's what makes this process so powerful.

This is why I always push back when people say, "Well, audiobooks don't count" or "Reading children's books isn't real reading." Who made up these rules? Who decided that understanding a story through listening is somehow less valid than reading words on a page? If I'm learning, and growing, and experiencing something new—then how is that not reading? If a children's book is what gets someone interested, why is that something to look down on? Reading isn't about proving yourself to other people. It's about what it gives you. And books—whether you read them, listen to them, or even discuss them—have the power to change lives.

Some of the most meaningful lessons don't come from dense, intellectual books that take weeks to get through—they come from stories that are simple, direct, and honest. And that's why children's books can be just as powerful for adults as they are for kids.

Take, for example, *Llama Llama Red Pajama*. At first glance, it's a read-aloud bedtime story, something light and playful that parents read to their children to help them wind down for the night. But when you pay attention, there's a deeper message.

It's a book about a baby llama who gets anxious when his mom leaves the room after tucking him in for the night. In the beginning he's a little worried, then gets more upset, and by the time she comes back, he's in a full-on meltdown. But what the book shows—what makes it so relatable—is that deep down, while the story is about bedtime, it's teaching children about patience, about learning to trust that even when you can't see the person you depend on, they're still there.

That hit me hard when I first read it. Because I know what it's like to feel abandoned, to panic when things don't go the way you thought they would, to feel like you don't have control. When I was younger, I didn't know how to name those feelings. So instead, I acted out. I lashed out. I got angry. And as an adult, I realized a lot of those feelings were still there—I had just learned to hide them better. I learned to push through things, to pretend I didn't care, to act like I had it all together. But that feeling? The sudden rush of fear, uncertainty, needing reassurance and not knowing if it's coming? It's not something you easily grow out of. Reading a book like *Llama Llama Red Pajama* made me see how universal those emotions are. It made me realize how sometimes, even as grown-ups, we're still the kid sitting in bed, scared that we're alone.

And this is why children's books count as so-called "real reading." Because what's more real than a book that makes you see yourself? That reminds you of something you've felt before but maybe never knew how to put into words? Some of the most powerful stories aren't the ones that challenge your intellect—they're the ones that speak to something deeper. They remind you of things you thought you'd forgotten, things that still shape the way you move through the world, even if you don't realize it.

When I was younger, I avoided books not only because I couldn't read them, but because they didn't feel like they were for me. They felt like things for other people, things I couldn't access. But when I was learning to read, I realized something: Books are for everyone. Stories are for everyone. And sometimes, books meant for kids do a better job of getting through to us than the ones meant for adults. Because they're honest. They don't dress things up or try to make them sound complicated. They say what they mean. And they meet you where you are.

For me, reading is all about feeling engaged in life and not just looking at it from the outside in. And children's books do that in a way that few other books can. They strip things down to their essence. They remind us of things we might have forgotten, things that got buried under the weight of growing up. And that's why I'll always believe that they're as valuable for adults as they are for kids.

Because sometimes, going back to the basics—going back to the stories that tell us it's okay to feel scared, that remind us we're not alone—is exactly what we need.

Every book I finish, no matter what it is, feels like another door opening. Each one teaches me something new about the world and about myself. I'll use *Percy Jackson* as an example again. The story is about a kid who finds out he's different from everyone else, that he has this incredible power he never knew about. But he also realizes that being different means having to navigate a world that wasn't built for him.

When you boil it down, there are a whole lot of books that communicate the same thing. It's a popular theme with books for kids, probably because it's a pretty universal truth for everyone.

That's exactly how I've felt my whole life. I had to figure out how to function in a world that wasn't made with someone like me in mind. I had to find my own tools, my own strategies, my own way of making it work.

What I want people to understand is there's no one right way to learn. There's no single path to success. What worked for someone else might not work for you, and that's okay. What matters is that you keep moving forward. Keep trying. Keep showing up for yourself.

And above all else, do *not* give up. Even when you desperately want to. Even when you think you're different, you're "not smart enough" to make it, or you don't have the support system you feel would make it easy for you. I know what it's like to feel like you're at the bottom of a mountain that's too high to climb. I know what it's like to sit there and think, "What's the point? I'll never be good at this." To believe deep down that you are different in a way that means you can't win, you can't keep up, you'll never get to where everyone else seems to be with ease.

Man, this cycle of self-blame is so normal. And you know what? You'll always feel this way if you let yourself sink into negativity. Because there's always a new goal as long as you keep going; there's always going to be a next level.

For a long time, I thought that learning to read would be the finish line. That once I cracked the code, everything else would fall into place. But now I know that this is only the beginning. There are so many things I still want to do. I want to read and write at an even higher level. I want to go to college. I want to stand on stages and speak to people who need to hear what I have to say. I want to be one of the greatest motivational speakers of all time. And every book I finish, every sentence I understand, every word I learn—it all gets me one step closer to my goals.

But none of this is just about me. It's about the people who see themselves in my story. The ones who were told they weren't smart enough, who felt like they had missed their chance, who thought they would never catch up. People beat by their parents, ignored by their teachers, lost in the system, whatever, man. All the bad things you can think of—people are going through it. I see them all the time, everywhere I go.

I see them because, in many ways, I was them. And now I want them to see what's possible. Together we can learn that everything is possible.

That's why I love my TikTok community so much. They remind me every day that I'm not alone. When I go Live, I see people who get it. People who have struggled, who have fought, who are still fighting. And together, we create something that goes beyond reading.

We build a space where people can learn without shame, where they can be vulnerable without fear.

And it's also why I'll never stop sharing my journey. Because I know there's another kid out there, another adult, another person who thinks they're too far behind to ever catch up. And I want them to know—it's never too late. You are not broken. You are not less than. You just need to find the tools that work for you. The biggest mistake you can make is to believe that because something is hard, it's impossible.

It's not.

Find a book, any book, and open it. And don't worry about whether it's the "right" book, or the "smart" book, or the book that other people think you should be reading. None of this matters (and if that kind of privacy does matter to you, get a book cover or read on an e-reader).

What matters the most is that you take the first step. Even if it's slow. Even if it's messy. Even if it feels pointless at first. Take your time. Let yourself struggle. Let yourself get frustrated. Let yourself fail. Let yourself be bad at it. Because every single time you sit down with a book, every time you push through even one page, even one paragraph, you're proving to yourself that you can do it. You're training your brain to push through the doubts, the discomfort, the parts where you want to give up.

You don't have to be perfect. You just have to keep going.

And I get it—it's frustrating when progress feels slow. It's frustrating when you look around and see other people who don't have to work as hard for the same thing. I used to sit there and wonder, why can't I be normal? Why can't I read like everyone else? But the thing is, that mindset keeps you stuck. You have to let go of the idea that your progress must look like anyone else's. It doesn't. It won't. But that doesn't mean it isn't happening.

Because here's what I know: Progress is sneaky. You don't wake up one morning and suddenly feel like you've transformed. It happens in small, almost invisible ways, in the moments where you decide to try again instead of giving up. It happens when you read a sentence that would have scared you six months ago, and now you understand it without even thinking. Or when you have the first feeling of believing in yourself a little more than you did yesterday.

And yeah, reading a hundred books in a year is a big goal. It's something that sounds impossible until you do it. But the real goal? It's getting up every day and doing the work. It's sitting down, even when you don't feel like it. Choosing to keep going, even when it's hard. Even when it's boring. Even when it feels like you're not getting anywhere.

And maybe no one else sees it yet. Maybe it doesn't feel like enough. But trust me—it is. It's like planting a seed. You don't see results right away. But underneath, things are shifting. Roots are growing. And one day, you look up and realize—you've built something real. You've created a version of yourself that you didn't even know was possible.

And that's what matters most.

So don't stop. Don't quit. Don't talk yourself out of the life that's waiting for you. Keep showing up. Keep trying. Keep proving to yourself, every single day, that you are capable of more than you ever imagined.

Because you are.

19

READING IS A MIRROR

Ishmael (1992), by Daniel Quinn

For most of my life, I thought my greatest secret was my inability to read. I assumed the hardest part would be admitting it, finally exposing the shame I had carried for so long. But sharing my story with the world taught me something unexpected: While honesty is about confession, it's also about living in that truth every single day. Reading became more than a skill to master; it became a mirror, reflecting the fears I had buried and the strength I never knew I had. Before, I had hidden behind avoidance and silence, but now, every word I read showed me a new version of myself, one I was still learning to recognize.

I didn't realize how deeply my illiteracy had shaped every part of my identity until I confronted it openly. As much relief as I felt coming clean, it also meant I had nowhere left to hide.

One of the biggest shocks for me after going public was how much daily life was still a challenge, even after people knew. Like I said before, even simple tasks like booking a hotel, scheduling flights, or keeping up with appointments remained out of my reach.

In movies and TV shows, once the guy figures out the root of his problem, all his other troubles melt away, like magic, and the hurdle is gone. I wish it was so easy.

In real life, identifying the problem tends to be just the first step. It wasn't as if revealing my illiteracy magically equipped me with the skills I'd missed out on for decades. I still faced constant limitations, only now they were visible to everyone.

The visibility I had, though empowering in many ways, also intensified all the complexities of each of my relationships. With Anne, my partner, the strain became even clearer once we both knew the full extent of my needs (which amounted to saying the full extent of her "duties" helping me).

As I discussed earlier, Anne had been forced into a role somewhere between partner, teacher, and personal assistant. As much as I hate to admit it, it was like she had to *parent* me. It wasn't fair to her, and I knew it. It wasn't her job to parent everyone in the house. The reality stung: Anne was taking on responsibilities she'd never asked for, simply because I couldn't manage daily life on my own. I was a drag on her. An anchor.

Acknowledging this imbalance in our relationship was painful. Before my story went public, we could both pretend things were more equal than they were. But once everything was out in the open, there was no going back. It hurt me deeply to realize that the people I loved most were paying the highest price for something I had no control over. It's easy to get into the blame-and-shame cycle. Breaking it required constant effort, patience, and humility on both our parts.

The emotional aspect of these limitations was often even harder than the practical difficulties. It had always been so tough for me to express love and appreciation clearly, something that should feel simple and natural. I'd forget to do things to show care and appreciation. It was a struggle to communicate sometimes, so I'd "accidentally" avoid it. This avoidance wasn't out of neglect or indifference. It was a defensive reaction, born from years of embarrassment and frustration. When communication itself is a struggle, it can feel easier to withdraw than to risk misunderstandings. But withdrawing didn't protect Anne—it left her feeling alone, unappreciated, and unsupported.

The pressure to overcome this pattern became even more intense once I began achieving some financial independence through my TikTok following. People ask me about this all the time and I'm sure there are books on it that could explain better than I can, but basically you can make money on TikTok if you treat it like a business, not just a hobby. The opportunities are there, but you have to know how to work them. The TikTok Creator Fund—which was revamped as the TikTok Creativity Program in 2023—is TikTok's way of paying creators for their content based on views. The more engagement you get—the more people who look at your videos and hit the like button and say something in the comments—the more you earn.

There are a bunch of other ways to earn money through TikTok, ranging from taking sponsorships, doing ads, and accepting tips from viewers and fans.

Obviously, no one goes on TikTok to be purposely boring; everyone there is trying to communicate their ideas or their jokes or whatever. When I first went on TikTok, it was to make fitness fun and advertise my business. I had no ideas about sponsorship, advertising, or any of that stuff. I was just being me.

In fact, if anything, I was playing it safe. It was never my plan to share too much about my private life, especially not the embarrassing parts. I never would have dreamed, back in the beginning, that I'd come out with my admission or that anyone would give a damn if I did.

All of this has been a complete shock to me.

And it's changed the way I live—I'm not nearly as worried and stressed out about money all the time the way I used to be.

Monetizing my posts gave me the means to contribute in tangible ways. For the first time, I could handle bills, purchase things we needed, and genuinely provide for Anne and our family. It felt incredible. Finally having the ability to pay some bills, to buy things for people—it was almost like my first real taste of independence. Yet, even as I enjoyed this newfound autonomy, I realized money alone wasn't enough to make for a fulfilling and happy life. The gaps in communication and emotional support remained. I could help financially, but emotional equality required deeper changes that no paycheck could buy.

What haunted me most about these realizations was reflecting on how I'd unintentionally hurt people in my past relationships. It wasn't ever my goal to cause pain, yet the ways I'd coped—lying, avoiding, becoming emotionally distant—left scars. These behaviors weren't random; they emerged from a desperate attempt to maintain some semblance of dignity and control when everything else felt chaotic. When people unintentionally hurt me, my warped sense of justice made me feel like I was secretly evening the score. I didn't understand at the time how harmful and self-defeating that pattern was.

In hindsight, it's clear my behavior was also fueled, at least in part, by envy. Watching others navigate the world easily, succeeding in everyday tasks that felt impossible for me, triggered resentment. They made me feel like less than I was, sometimes just by being themselves. It looked to me like some people cruised through the world with what looked to me like extreme ease.

Well, lucky them, but it didn't seem fair to me. I resented being on the low rungs of the ladder.

That resentment, born out of pain and frustration more than reality, twisted into something toxic. It drove me to sabotage relationships with people who genuinely cared for me, all in the misguided attempt to protect myself from deeper hurt.

But uncovering the reasons behind my past actions didn't instantly heal the damage I'd done. Opening up about illiteracy and my struggles provided context, but context alone didn't cushion or erase past wounds. Maybe I thought that telling people the truth about illiteracy and everything else would . . . fix things. It didn't, of course. It just meant that people knew what I was doing, where I was coming from. Transparency was the first step in a much longer journey of repair. Anne and others finally saw clearly who I was, but we had to confront all the hurtful behaviors and habits I'd built up over the years.

This painful confrontation brought with it another difficult truth: Not everyone would—or could—stay with me through the process of healing and change. Relationships that had been strained by years of misunderstandings, miscommunications, and hurt wouldn't automatically be healed just because I'd finally explained myself. Not everybody is gonna make it to the finish line with me, if there is one. And that's okay. Anne is a grown woman; it isn't her responsibility to teach me basic life skills or constantly reassure me. Part of my growth was understanding that relationships aren't only about love—they're also about fairness, reciprocity, and respect for one another's limits.

Recognizing and facing these truths head-on required bravery that went far beyond admitting I couldn't read. The real bravery was in choosing to stay present, to listen to how my actions had impacted others, and to commit to learning new ways of living and loving—even when it was deeply uncomfortable. I wasn't sure I had it in me to succeed. I was forced to confront who I had been, who I wanted to become, and how far I still had to go.

As I moved deeper into the process of change, I realized how ingrained my old habits were, and how much more complicated it was going to be to untangle them. Learning to read had seemed like the biggest obstacle, but as it turned out, it was just the first layer I had to peel back.

Beneath the surface struggle lay decades of learned behaviors, self-protective mechanisms, and emotional reflexes that had defined my relationships. I had spent my life feeling inadequate, incapable, and dependent—feelings that had seeped into every interaction, every argument, every quiet moment of frustration between Anne and me. Addressing these deeper patterns meant relearning everything I thought I knew about myself and my connections to others.

No grown adult, especially a partner, should have to tell me when I'm doing the right thing or remind me when I'm doing the wrong thing. I'm supposed to know that stuff. I had spent years unintentionally placing Anne, and plenty of others, in the position of caretaker, leaning on their strength and patience without even fully realizing it. Now that I could see it clearly, I understood the unfairness. It was a weight no one should have to carry.

As I built new habits and confronted these uncomfortable truths, I found myself facing an unexpected form of loneliness. While Anne supported me unconditionally, the road toward becoming emotionally independent was mine alone to navigate. No matter how much she wanted to help, there were parts of my journey she couldn't walk for me. It was hard, isolating, and occasionally overwhelming, yet it was a necessary stage of growth.

The progress wasn't linear, either. For every moment of clarity and growth, there were equally frustrating setbacks. Just because I'm on this journey of self-discovery doesn't mean I always have the time or space for it. It's not like I stopped needing to work; it's not like my kids stopped growing. No, I've had to roll with those punches. Even when I'm not equipped to. Life didn't pause to let me catch up, and that relentless pace tested my resilience. I'd learned to read, yes, but to some extent, it now meant that the world expected more from me now. Responsibilities didn't go away simply because I was still learning to handle them. There was constant pressure, not only from external sources, but internally as well—to keep improving, to keep showing up, and to avoid falling back into the comfortable patterns of dependency.

One of the harshest realities I grappled with was the impact my illiteracy had on my ability to communicate effectively. It's terrible, because I want everyone I've ever been with to feel loved, connected, safe. I want them to feel what they helped me feel: like someone is on their side. But I did not have the tools, the language, and the emotional intelligence to convey all this clearly. Learning those skills took practice, patience, and humility—qualities I was still developing.

Yet amid all the struggles and setbacks, I began to find glimpses of real growth. *And it felt great!* I don't want, for a minute, to lose that in the shuffle of woes and challenges I went through, because we *all* have woes and challenges—what they are depends on where they spring from.

The word *growth* in terms of living a better life used to sound like dry, dull work to me. It sounded like a task, no fun at all. Maybe you know what I mean. If so, I'm here to tell you that growth in the sense of gaining knowledge and moving through the world with more self-confidence feels incredible. The ability to form plans for your own life, to draw a blueprint of exactly what you want to do and achieve, is a gift.

Being able to follow that blueprint and achieve levels of success you used to think were only for "the lucky ones" or other people is an *incredible* feeling.

This is what I'm talking about when I say you need to work hard for growth but it's worth it.

If you're lucky, you're constantly growing. So don't sell yourself the story that once you overcome one hurdle you're finished. As I've said, you're not finished as long as you're alive. Once again, this is not to discourage you but to remind you, as you continue along your own path, that feeling like you can't do it, even feeling like you've had a setback, is all part of the program.

The best news is that sometimes the parts you fear the most turn out to be a piece of cake.

Being honest about my needs and limitations didn't isolate me as I'd feared; instead, it connected me more deeply to Anne, our kids, and even to myself. Anne and I made a point of communicating openly about the practical adjustments we needed to make. Instead of silently assuming she would handle everything, I began explicitly asking for help when necessary, then making clear plans to handle tasks myself in the future. This transparent honesty about what I could and couldn't do created space for genuine partnership. It allowed Anne to step back from constant caretaking and trust that I was genuinely committed to growing, rather than simply relying on her forever.

Over time, I saw the strain lift from her shoulders as I took on more responsibilities, communicated openly, and became a genuine partner rather than someone who constantly relied on her care. It wasn't perfect—we still had misunderstandings and tough days—but now we were navigating them together, openly and honestly. There was room for both of us to be imperfect, to ask for help, and to grow side by side.

The TikTok following I'd built became instrumental in this process of transformation. At first, it was just a way to share my life, or at least the story I was willing to put out there. It then evolved into a source of accountability and community. They're my community now, you know? If I'm feeling lonely or sad, and want a drink or something (which I gave up a while back), I can go Live and someone will be there to talk me down.

And then I'm there with all these people, and we're doing what I always wanted to be doing. The honest-to-god truth is that I love reading, I love books, I love stories, and I love talking about all of those things with the community that has been encouraging me through this.

Social media has become not just a platform for my reading, but an essential part of it. It has reinforced my commitment, reminded me I wasn't alone, and encouraged me to stay authentic and vulnerable—even when vulnerability felt scary.

That relationship with my followers has also helped me improve my communication skills in a safe, supportive environment. Reading their comments live and interacting with them forced me to confront my limitations head-on and in real time. But instead of feeling judged or inadequate, I was met with patience and kindness. And they worked with me, resending comments if I missed them the first time, which is easy to do even if you're a great reader because they scroll by fast.

My online community has been patient with me. And I know some of them personally now. I consider them actual real-life friends, which is so cool. The same people will get on my Live and talk to me again, and I'll remember them. It became a testing ground for practicing genuine dialogue—something I could then apply to my personal relationships. The skills I built online shaped my interactions at home, improving how I communicated my needs, my feelings, and my appreciation for Anne.

Perhaps most importantly, TikTok provided a space for unconditional acceptance from those around me—a space that was often missing in my own inner dialogue. It almost felt like unconditional love. And this is what I—like probably everybody—want. Having such immediate, visible support reminded me that my worth wasn't defined by my shortcomings or past mistakes. It reinforced the idea that my value was inherent, not contingent upon how quickly I mastered reading or how easily I handled life's practicalities. It was a powerful realization, one that gradually reshaped my self-perception and how I interacted with others.

The only time I ever had a community like this was when I was a kid and spent the long afternoons and evenings at the local Boys & Girls Club. I don't know what I would have done without it. My mom was working, my dad wasn't around, and here was this place where I could go and be supported. It couldn't replace family or a good education, of course, but it was a safe place to be, and I think it's the thing that made me learn how to be a human. I got to know other kids like me and I got to know kids not like me. I learned to play basketball, dodgeball, Ping-Pong, four-square, *breakdancing*—I learned breakdancing there! It was kinda like social media is today. Somewhere, there's a corner where someone is doing something or talking about something you don't know about or you want to know about, and you can go spend time there. There were nice adults who could help you out if you needed it. Nice kids who were there even when it was embarrassing—like the time at swimming when I got pantsed and another kid helped me out, even when everyone else was laughing.

In a way, finding friends on social media these days is like that to me. They make it easier to grow, to see myself clearly, and to help me find who and what I want to be next.

Your place in the world depends on who you are as a person. What's inside and how you conduct yourself with others. If you're honest about who you are, all this falls into place without you even having to think about it. It's a beautiful thing and I never dreamed it would be my life.

By the midpoint of this transformation, it became clear that genuine growth required more than just learning to read—it required me to rebuild my identity. I needed to cultivate honesty, humility, and vulnerability as daily practices. I had to confront my flaws without succumbing to shame and accept help without letting it erode my sense of independence. More than anything, I learned to recognize that real partnership isn't about perfection; it's about willingness—willingness to be accountable, to be patient, and to embrace discomfort as part of the journey toward something better.

But even with these realizations, my journey was far from over. Every step forward revealed new complexities, new challenges, and new opportunities for growth. I was beginning to understand that genuine transformation involves continuously choosing to move forward, even when the path ahead is uncertain.

Sometimes, the road isn't fun. There were times when I was like, *Wow, my life is actually worse than before.* At first, I was broke, anxious, and more aware of my own issues than ever. But those moments of doubt and struggle were crucial components of genuine change. I had to recognize and confront the parts of myself I'd avoided for so long. And even though facing those truths was painful, every step was essential.

The people who joined me on social media have actively participated in my journey. They send messages, share stories, and offer encouragement. Many people have messaged me about their struggles. Many told me that they, too, couldn't read. Learning to read helped me find these people. Connecting with them was inspiring and healing. We were forging new ground together, reshaping how we saw ourselves, our potential, and the value we placed on our own lives.

Through this community, I found a space to openly admit that I was still learning, still struggling with day-to-day things, and that it was okay. My honesty gave others permission to do the same, and in that shared vulnerability, we found strength. This community reminded me every day that being courageous wasn't about avoiding failure—it was about openly accepting it as part of the path to success.

At the same time, I also learned to separate my past from my present, something I struggled with deeply at first. It's so hard, but so important to remember. There's so much chatter about not playing the victim, about not blaming others, about being strong. But real strength comes from recognizing the ways you've been failed and hurt, acknowledging the wounds you still carry, and making peace with them. For me, I gained the understanding that while I wasn't responsible for everything that had happened to me, I had the power and responsibility to choose what came next.

I finally understood that being kind to myself was just as important as learning to read or becoming more independent. The more compassionate I became with myself, the easier it became to extend that compassion to Anne, my kids, and my community. I was able to cultivate a new way of being in the world, one marked by empathy, patience, and genuine respect for the challenges we all face.

In this evolving sense of self-awareness, I also realized that growth didn't have a finish line. This wasn't a project that would end once I'd read a certain number of books or mastered certain tasks. Instead, it was a lifelong commitment to showing up for myself and others every day, to continuously embrace discomfort and uncertainty as essential parts of the journey.

As I looked ahead, my vision shifted away from survival and toward creating something lasting, something meaningful that could outlive my own journey. I imagined a world with resources designed for people like me—accessible reading tools, cooking guides, adaptive shopping apps, places where struggling readers could thrive without shame. I wanted the things I'd learned through pain and struggle to smooth the path for someone else, to help them avoid feeling alone, lost, or inadequate.

In the end, the biggest lesson I want to share is about hope. Hope that my story, with all its ups and downs, might inspire someone else to take the first difficult step toward their own transformation. Because the truth is, every step of the journey is worth it. Every struggle, every mistake, every victory—it's all part of becoming the person I always hoped I could be. And as long as I continue taking those steps forward, I know I'm exactly where I need to be.

Reading is a mirror, reflecting to us more than words on the page but also our own beliefs, struggles, and evolving understanding of the world. When I finally learned to read, I began seeing myself more clearly, recognizing my own patterns, limitations, and potential. *Ishmael*, by Daniel Quinn, is one of those books that held up an especially powerful mirror for me. It's a philosophical novel about a gorilla "teacher" who telepathically communicates with a man—his "student"—about humanity and civilization. The idea of the story—that we are shaped by the stories we've been told and the ones we tell ourselves—resonated deeply. Just as the narrator in *Ishmael* is forced to confront the invisible myths that have defined his worldview, I had to look closely at the internal rules I'd lived by—the ones that told me I was incapable, broken, or destined to be dependent. Learning to read opened up a new way of seeing my life, my relationships, and my own power to change my story.

In *Ishmael*, the main character comes to realize that the world he has always accepted as reality is merely an idea—a story passed down through generations. Reading, in the same way, forces us to examine the stories we've internalized about ourselves. Before I could read, I accepted a version of myself that felt small and incapable, a narrative I hadn't written but had somehow absorbed. But with each book I devoured, I saw more of myself reflected, challenging those things I took as truth. Like the narrator in *Ishmael*, I began to understand that I wasn't stuck to my old stories—I could rewrite them. Reading didn't just give me knowledge; it gave me the power to see myself, to understand my own identity, and eventually, hopefully—with a lot of work—make substantial changes so that I like who I see when I truly look at myself.

20

READING IS THE BEGINNING

The Track Series (2017–25), by Jason Reynolds

If there's one thing I want people to take away from this book, it's that the journey is yours. Your path, your progress, your growth—it all belongs to you, and no one else can dictate what it should look like. And we can, without shame, ask for help if we need it. We spend so much time comparing ourselves to others, thinking we need to be at a certain level before we can even think about moving forward, but the truth is, there is no scale. There's no universal standard for how your journey is supposed to go. There's only where you are, where you want to be, and the steps you take to get there.

When I first tried learning to read, I didn't have that confidence. I thought reading was something other people did—people who were naturally smart, people who had been doing it their whole lives. Not me. I thought I wasn't qualified. And this is the same mindset that keeps so many people from even trying in the first place. If you think you must be great at something before you can even begin, you'll never get anywhere at all.

You don't have to be perfect. You don't have to be the best. You just have to do it. It's about doing it all, for your life. Doing and being who you want. And you must trust that wherever you are, it's enough.

The biggest shift in my life came when I finally realized that I don't have to measure myself against anyone else's standards. I don't have to read like someone else. I don't have to succeed like someone else. I don't have to live like someone else. My journey is mine, and the only thing that matters is that I keep moving forward.

And that's true for you too.

Believe me, whatever you're facing, whatever you think is holding you back, know that it doesn't define you. Don't let it! Don't trap yourself in a cage made of someone else's expectations or doubts. Everything you do goes down as part of your path. Everyone has struggles, doubts, and moments where they think *I can't do this* but those things aren't roadblocks—they're stepping stones.

They're lessons.

Proof that you're growing.

Boy, I wish someone had sat me down and told me this when I was younger. I wish someone had looked me in the eye and said, "You are enough, just as you are." It took me a long time to understand that for myself, but now that I do, I want to make sure no one else has to wait as long as I did to hear it.

You don't have to know everything up front. You don't have to have it all figured out. You just have to be willing to take the first step. And then another. And then another. And before you know it, you'll look back and realize how far you've come.

This seems like the right place to confide one last story. Almost two years ago, I had a mental health breakdown. I'd been battling with mental health all my life—with my OCD, anxiety, and PTSD. And I'm dealing with all this stuff that I'm going through, working through it with my therapist, and it's great now, really, but let's go back to how the breakdown happened.

One night it all got to be too much for me. Not just the reading, all of it. The past, relationships, parenting, trying to navigate a difficult world. I pretty much lost all sense of myself and stripped down naked (if you recall my story in chapter 11 as a fourteen-year-old, stripping off my clothes seems to be consistently symbolic for me), ran outside my apartment, and started punching the wall of the building. I was so tired of being trapped in my own mind and not knowing what to do. I ended up punching that wall for, I don't know, I want to say a good fifteen to twenty minutes, maybe even longer, because I was punching it until the cops came and tased me.

This was not my proudest moment and I almost didn't include it here at all. I was fully naked, punching a wall in public, someone called the cops, and they came and tased me. Bear in mind, I don't remember any of it, but I got the story from the police. The only thing I remember is stripping down naked.

When I became conscious again, I was in the hospital, handcuffed to the bed, and my hands were completely torn apart, bloody and ripped up from punching the rough texture of the wall. From there I was sent to the county jail. Even though it was obviously a mental health emergency, I was also considered a danger to the public.

I was in the county jail for three days. Still naked. They gave me something to wear from the hospital but it was a sheet kind of thing, like a hospital gown, made out of paper. That's all I had on for three days in prison. No shoes either, so I ended up using sandwich bags from some of the people who were in the holding cell with me. I was a mess. They finally bandaged me up and put me into a single room for people with mental health issues.

After that, I was sent home but I was still kind of lost in myself. So I checked myself into a mental hospital for three more days. When I got out, I started reading books on mental health.

Reading books now took on a new importance because I wanted to get therapy but I didn't have access. Meanwhile, my relationship with Anne was falling apart and I was stressed from parenting and doing a pretty bad job of it. I was like, man, I need to change my life. I need to figure something out.

Being able to read about my conditions enabled me to get the help that I needed. As I read, I felt like, oh my gosh, this is me. I need to get this type of help. Eventually I got two therapists and that has really, really helped me. I'm in such a great place now with handling my mental illnesses and anxieties. This is important: I honestly don't know if I'd be here if I hadn't been able to read my way into helping myself.

I was embarrassed to share this at first. But, hey, all of this was embarrassing once. If I can help even one person by admitting I went through this and found my way out, it's worth it.

In your own way, and with your own challenges, fighting through to the other side will be worth it for you too. Take your time. Trust yourself. Be patient with your growth. And most importantly, don't be afraid to write your own story.

And that's what I want for you—to know that no matter where you are in your life, you are allowed to grow and if you try you literally won't be able to stop it. No matter what the map looks like or how much energy you have for it, you can do it. Learn at your own pace. You are allowed to figure things out as you go. And you don't have to wait for permission. If I had waited until I felt ready, I never would have gotten anywhere. If I'd waited until I thought I could be the best at reading, I wouldn't be writing this book right now. Because there is no one who is the best at reading!

I know people look at me now and think what I'm doing is inspiring, but I'm not doing anything that you can't do. I'm not special. I just made the decision to succeed, and I refused to stop. That's all it is. If you're waiting for a sign, for someone to tell you that it's okay to go after what you want, this is it. This is your sign. Start now, exactly as you are, and believe that you belong.

I never thought I'd be able to read a book, let alone write one. But here I am. And if I can do it, so can you. You've got to believe me. No matter where you are right now, no matter what you've been through, no matter how impossible it seems—you are capable. You are enough. And you always have been.

That's the truth. You don't need to wait until you're better, smarter, stronger. You are ready now. Take a step, even if it's small. Even if it feels insignificant. Because every step you take shapes your story. And one day, you'll look back and realize that the hardest part wasn't the journey itself—it was believing that you were allowed to take it, deserving of it, in the first place.

There was a time when people who needed glasses were mocked. It's funny to think about now, but back then, the first people wearing glasses must have felt exposed, different, maybe even ashamed. They probably tried to hide it, probably hated putting them on, because the world around them hadn't yet caught up to the reality that some people needed a little extra help to see. And now? It's nothing. It's a nonissue. Glasses are fashionable. People wear them just for style. You can walk into any store and buy reading glasses off the shelf. Nobody points or laughs. Nobody questions it. You need glasses? You get glasses. Simple.

Yeah, some jerk kids are still getting some mileage out of the old *four-eyes* insult, but that's irrelevant. Kids will be mean about anything.

I want people without great education to become more accepted. There's a huge population who has been underserved by the education system. But there's still so much shame around being able to ask for help. As if it says something about our character to not just . . . already *know* everything? There's so much shame associated with having needs, with needing help. It might be the kid who's falling behind in class and is too embarrassed to ask for help. The person ordering at a drive-through hesitates because they're scared they might get the words wrong. The guy at the bank pretends to understand the paperwork he's signing because asking for help makes him feel small.

But what if that changed? What if we reached a point where someone could say, "Hold on, let me grab my reader," and nobody blinked? Where technology, tools, accommodations, and basic human patience made it so normal that nobody ever had to feel like they didn't belong? What if we accepted that some people get left behind by this flawed world we've built? What if we made it okay to go back and get them?

What if more people could say, "Oh, I don't get the reference," or "Could you explain that to me?"

I want people to stop looking at reading, and all learning, like it's a pass/fail situation. Like either you can do it, or you can't, and if you can't, you're screwed. That's not how anything in life works. It's not how intelligence works. It's not how growth works. Nobody questions whether a person with bad eyesight deserves to see. Or whether a person with a prosthetic leg deserves to walk. So why do we question whether someone who struggles with reading deserves access to the same world of information as everybody else? Why do we make people feel like they're defective if they need a different way in?

I want kids to grow up knowing that reading doesn't have to look one way. Just because it's hard for them doesn't mean they're broken. Maybe the way we've been teaching reading isn't the only way to do it. I want the kid sitting in class, frustrated and feeling like they'll never catch up, to know that their brain isn't the problem—the system is. I want the adult who's been hiding their struggle for decades to know that it's never too late, that their worth isn't tied to how well they can read a paragraph on a page. I want people to see that the future is in making sure everyone has access to the tools to help them thrive in a way that works for them. I want to take away the shame. I want to take away the fear. I want to make it normal.

I do what I do publicly because I want people to see it, to know what's possible. If someone out there sees me taking my time, asking for help, maybe they'll think, *If he can do it, I can do it too.* And this is only the beginning. The tools we have now? The awareness we have now? This is just the first step. In twenty, thirty years, I want to see a world where nobody gets laughed at for learning in a different way. Where kids don't feel scared to raise their hands and ask for help. Where the guy at the drive-through, the person at the bank, the student in the classroom—where nobody has to pretend to be something they're not just to get by.

I imagine a world where kids grow up seeing different ways to learn the same way they see different ways to get around. Some people walk, some ride bikes, others drive, and still others use wheelchairs. But everybody moves. That's what reading should be. Some people read with their eyes. Some listen. Some people use readers or special fonts or take longer to process. But everybody reads. Everybody learns. Everybody moves forward in their own way.

I hope this book can be part of that shift; that it can help someone realize they are not alone. That whatever they're struggling with, there's a way through it. That the way they've been told to do things isn't the only way things *can* be done. That they get to define what success looks like for them.

I didn't start this journey thinking I was going to change the world. I just wanted to change my world. But as I've grown, and learned, as I've seen how many people relate to my story, I realize now that maybe I can be part of something bigger. Maybe someday a kid will pick up this book, read my story, and feel something they never felt before.

Hope.

Hope that no matter where they are, or what they're struggling with, no matter how impossible it feels, they can find their way forward. They can learn. And grow. And most importantly, they are not alone.

I know what it feels like to be alone. I know what it feels like to believe you're too far behind, that you missed your chance, that the world has already decided your fate for you. But it's not real. It's not the truth. The only thing that decides your fate is you. The only thing that can hold you back is the belief that you can't move forward.

If I had let these beliefs win, I never would have even tried reading. I never would have shared my story. I never would have found this incredible community of people who support me, who push me, who remind me every single day that I'm not in this alone. And neither are you.

Learning doesn't stop just because you didn't get it right the first time. Growth doesn't have an expiration date. There is no point in life where you are required to give up on yourself. If you're still breathing, you still have time to change, to heal, to build the life you want. It won't always be easy. Sometimes, it will feel impossible. But just because something is hard doesn't mean it isn't worth doing.

The only difference between the people who succeed and the people who don't isn't talent or intelligence or luck. It's the decision to keep going. To believe in something even when there's no proof yet. To bet on yourself.

And if you do, I promise, the world will open up in ways you never imagined.

Just like it did for me.

I wanted to end here with one more recommendation: The Track series by Jason Reynolds, which has four books, with a fifth one set to come out in October 2025.

This series is important to me because it tells the stories of kids who are trying to figure things out—kids who are dealing with real struggles, real emotions, and real-life situations while also trying to do something as simple as run track. These kids are carrying the weight of their real lives, even at a young age. The things happening at home, the way they show up in the world, and how it all affects the way they move through their day-to-day lives. And that's something I deeply understand.

When I think back to being a teenager, I think about how much I was holding in, how much I had to navigate without the right tools or guidance. People saw me as the angry kid, the kid who was always getting into trouble. On the outside, that's what it looked like. But what they didn't see was the full picture. They didn't see the struggle at home, the stress, the feeling of being lost in a system that wasn't built for me. They didn't see how badly I wanted to belong, to be good at something, to have a space where I felt safe. I didn't even know how to put those feelings into words at the time. I acted out because it was the only way I knew how to express myself.

And that's why these books hit so hard. They show kids like me—kids who have a lot going on under the surface, kids who are misunderstood, kids who want to do the right thing but sometimes don't know how. The characters in Track remind me of myself and so many other kids I knew growing up. They remind me that struggling doesn't mean you're a bad kid. It just means you're a kid who's trying to figure things out in a world that doesn't always give you the space to do that.

I played sports too, like the kids in these books. I played basketball, and I loved it. But my anger got in the way. I got kicked off my ninth-grade basketball team after cussing out my coach. At the time, I couldn't explain what was going on inside me. I knew that basketball was one of the only things I had, and when it felt like it was being taken away, I lashed out. My coach probably thought I was being disrespectful, just another troublemaker who didn't appreciate the opportunity. But the truth was, I didn't know how to process my emotions. I didn't know how to say, "Basketball is the one thing in my life that makes sense right now. Please don't take it away from me." Instead, I exploded. And then I was out.

That's the reality for so many kids. People expect them to just behave, to follow the rules, to do well in school, but they don't stop to ask what's going on in their lives. They don't realize that the kid who won't sit still in class might not have had anything to eat that morning. Or that the kid who refuses to do his homework might not have anyone at home who can help him with it. And the kid getting into fights might not be angry at his classmates—he might be angry at the world. And when nobody sees that, when nobody tries to understand, those kids come to *believe* what everyone says about them. That they're just trouble. That they'll never be anything more than that.

This is why books like the Track series matter. Because they tell the truth. They don't just show kids as one thing. They show the layers, the complexity, the struggle beneath the surface. They show the way coaches, teachers, and parents all play a role, how their own lives and struggles impact the kids they're trying to help. When you're a kid, you don't always realize that adults are dealing with their own problems. You don't think about what your coach might be going through, what your mom might be carrying. You only see your world, your problems, your pain. And that's fair. But books like these help bridge that gap. They help kids see beyond themselves, and they help adults understand the kids they're trying to reach.

When I look back, I wish I'd been able to read this series when I was young. I wish I had seen characters who were going through what I was going through, who made me feel like I wasn't alone. Maybe then I would have understood myself a little better. Maybe then I would have known that I wasn't just some bad kid—I was a kid who needed support, a kid who needed tools and who needed to believe that he was more than his mistakes.

Stories don't just entertain us—they show us what's possible. They help us see ourselves in a new way, reminding us that we are not alone in our experiences, our fears, our dreams. A book is more than words on a page; it's a mirror, a window, a doorway. It can reflect who we are, show us a world we never imagined, or offer us a way forward when we thought we had nowhere left to go.

When I was a kid, I didn't have characters I could see myself in. And because of that, I didn't believe I had a future beyond what I could see right in front of me. But now, I know better. Now, I know that the right story at the right time can change everything. It can plant a seed, open a door, shift a perspective. And sometimes, it can save a life.

It's never too late to change your story, to rewrite the narrative that has been placed on you, to step into the life you deserve. No matter where you are, or what you've been through, you are not stuck. You are not defined by your past. You are not limited by what you thought was possible. You can always grow, always learn, always move forward.

And if nothing else, I hope this book proves that. I hope it shows that learning to read at thirty-four years old isn't a failure—it's a victory. That struggling is the proof that you haven't given up. That asking for help, taking your time, doing things your own way—none of that makes you any less worthy. It only makes you human.

This isn't the end of my story. It's just the beginning. And if you're reading this, wherever you are in your own journey, I hope you know that the story is never over.

We're the authors.

And there is always another chapter waiting to be written.

THE BEGINNING

ACKNOWLEDGMENTS

I want to thank M. P. Henry first, thank you for your patience, dedication, and all the hard work you've poured into this process. Your creativity and commitment made this journey smoother and more meaningful than I could've imagined.

Special thanks to the teams at Union Square & Co.—executive editor Barbara Berger, project editor Alison Skrabek, creative director Lisa Forde, art director and jacket designer Patrick Sullivan, interior designer Rich Hazelton, and production manager Sandy Noman; also thanks to copyeditor Diane Joao. And to Lauren Spieler, Steve Troha, and the Folio team—thank you for believing in my work and taking a chance to help me find the right home for my book. Your support opened doors I couldn't have reached on my own, and I'm deeply grateful.

To my sister—thank you for stepping in like a second mother when I needed it most. You helped keep me grounded when I was younger, and your guidance meant more than I ever said out loud.

To my mother—regardless of the obstacles we had along the way, please know that the man I am today is because of you. You fought with everything you had to shape me into someone strong, kind, and grounded. Life wasn't always perfect but the good outweighed the bad, and your love was always at the center of it. Without you, I simply wouldn't be who I am. I'll carry that truth with me, always.

Anne Halkias—thank you for being and doing so much more than I could ever try to put into words. You have championed me through so much, honestly, this wouldn't have even gotten done without you. I couldn't have asked for a better teammate.

To my two boys, thank you for showing me every day what it truly means to be a father. You inspire me, teach me, and fill my heart with pride and love.

I also want to thank the social media community—especially TikTok—for being the best community anywhere and for being the supportive teachers I never had as a youngster. The knowledge, wisdom, encouragement, and even tough love I've received from you helped guide me in ways I didn't know I needed. You've made a real difference in my life.

And last but not least, to you—you know who you are. Whether we speak today or not, I love every single one of you. Each of you, in your own way, played a part in helping me become the person I am today. There are so many kids and adults out there who shared the same struggles I did, and to you, I say this: I hope this book becomes your motivation. Keep going. Keep pushing. Thank *you*.

RECOMMENDATIONS

NOTE: The books are listed here in the general order in which they were read.

The 100+ Books I Read in One Year

365 Quotes to Live Your Life By by I. C. Robledo

The Diary of a Young Girl by Anne Frank

The Giving Tree by Shel Silverstein

The Giver by Lois Lowry

Fish in a Tree by Lynda Mullaly Hunt

I Am Every Good Thing by Derrick Barnes, illustrated by Gordon C. James

The Outsiders by S. E. Hinton

Greatest Inspirational Quotes: 365 Days to More Happiness, Success, and Motivation by Joe Tichio

Percy Jackson and the Olympians: The Lightning Thief by Rick Riordan

The Book of Jose: A Memoir by Fat Joe with Shaheem Reid

The Witches by Roald Dahl, illustrated by Quentin Blake

Recover Today from OCD and Intrusive Thoughts by Christopher J. Lopez

Goodnight Moon by Margaret Wise Brown, pictures by Clement Hurd

Who Wants a Cheap Rhinoceros? by Shel Silverstein

Danny Dollar, Millionaire Extraordinaire: The Lemonade Escapade by Ty Allan Jackson

The Story of Ferdinand by Munro Leaf, drawings by Robert Lawson

House Arrest by K. A. Holt

Corduroy by Don Freeman

The Very Hungry Caterpillar by Eric Carle

You Owe You: Ignite Your Power, Your Purpose, and Your Why by Eric Thomas, PhD

The Supadupa Kid by Ty Allan Jackson

Chicken Little adapted by Mara Alperin, illustrated by Nick East

A Bad Case of Stripes by David Shannon

Let's Go for a Drive! by Mo Willems

A Little Book About Books: Quotes for the Bibliophile in Your Life by Orange Hippo

A Day with No Words by Tiffany Hammond, illustrated by Kate Cosgrove

This Is Not My Hat by Jon Klassen

Everyone's a Aliebn When Ur a Aliebn Too: A Book by Jomny Sun

Some of My Best Friends: And Other White Lies I've Been Told by Tajja Isen

My Brother Is My Brother! by Leslie Clark, illustrated by Ilma Salman

Kindness Rocks by Sonica Ellis, illustrated by Fx and Color Studio

Love You Forever by Robert Munsch, illustrated by Sheila McGraw

The Day the Crayons Quit by Drew Daywalt, pictures by Oliver Jeffers

David Goes to School by David Shannon

No, David! by David Shannon

If You Give a Mouse a Cookie by Laura Numeroff, illustrated by Felicia Bond

The Smallest Spot of a Dot: The Little Ways We're Different, the Big Ways We're the Same by Linsey Davis and Michael Tyler, illustrated by Lucy Fleming

Pokémon: The Rescue Mission by Maria S. Barbo

I Am a Baby by Bob Shea

Duck & Goose by Tad Hills

The Original Curious George by H. A. Rey and Margret Rey

I Feel That: A Quote Collection for All the Feels by Christina Scotch

A Little Book About Books: Quotes for the Bibliophile in Your Life by Orange Hippo *(re-read)*

The Four Agreements: A Practical Guide to Personal Freedom by Don Miguel Ruiz

I Hate Reading: How to Read When You'd Rather Not by Beth Bacon

The Phantom Tollbooth by Norton Juster, illustrated by Jules Feiffer

Holes by Louis Sachar

Dirty Laundry: Why Adults with ADHD Are So Ashamed and What We Can Do to Help by Richard Pink and Roxanne Emery

Be the Grapes by Tami Fitzkoff, illustrations by Kathlene Linehan

Master Your Emotions: A Practical Guide to Overcome Negativity and Better Manage Your Feelings by Thibaut Meurisse

A Kids Book About Imagination by LeVar Burton

The Rhino Who Swallowed a Storm by LeVar Burton and Susan Schaefer Bernardo, illustrations by Courtenay Fletcher

Look Up with Me: Neil deGrasse Tyson: A Life Among the Stars by Jennifer Berne, illustrations by Lorraine Nam

Charlotte's Web by E. B. White, illustrated by Garth Williams

Mirabelle's Metamorphosis by Sharon Rask-Huntington

Zella, Zack, and Zodiac by Bill Peet

The Cat in the Hat by Dr. Seuss

Think About Someone You Love by Dallas Clayton

Max and the Tag-Along Moon by Floyd Cooper

Winnie-the-Pooh: Pooh Goes Visiting by A. A. Milne, with decorations by E. H. Shepard

Winnie-the-Pooh: Eeyore Has a Birthday by A. A. Milne, with decorations by E. H. Shepard

Green Eggs and Ham by Dr. Seuss

V Is for Vegan: The ABCs of Being Kind by Ruby Roth

Exploring Souls: The Art of Understanding Who We Really Are by Adrian Gabriel Dumitru

Yes, I'm Not Okay: Helpful Quotes About Depression by Kelly Smith

It's Never Too Late by Kathie Lee Gifford

Winnie-the-Pooh: Piglet Meets a Heffalump by A. A. Milne, with decorations by E. H. Shepard

My Shadow Is Purple by Scott Stuart

Where the Wild Things Are by Maurice Sendak

Black Gold: The Story of Oil in Our Lives by Albert Marrin

A Giraffe and a Half by Shel Silverstein

The Missing Piece by Shel Silverstein

The Magic in Oliver! – A personalized book created by I See Me! press

Knockout by K. A. Holt

Leo the Late Bloomer by Robert Kraus, pictures by Jose Aruego

Last Week Tonight with John Oliver Presents: A Day in the Life of Marlon Bundo by Marlon Bundo with Jill Twiss, illustrated by EG Keller

The Very Quiet Cricket by Eric Carle

Better Together: The ABCs of Building Social Skills and Friendships by Dr. Melissa Munro Boyd, illustrated by Vanessa Alexandre

Stone Soup – adapted from a folk tale (multiple versions)

Llama Llama Red Pajama by Anna Dewdney

10 Little Fingers and 10 Little Toes by Mem Fox, illustrated by Helen Oxenbury

Rabbityness by Jo Empson

The Body Keeps the Score: Brain, Mind, and Body in the Healing of Trauma by Bessel van der Kolk, MD

8 Things Every Boy Should Know About Being a Man by Horace Hough

The Pivot Year: 365 Days to Become the Person You Truly Want to Be by Brianna Wiest

101 Essays That Will Change the Way You Think by Brianna Wiest

Ishmael by Daniel Quinn

The Track Series by Jason Reynolds

The Power of Now: A Guide to Spiritual Enlightenment by Eckhart Tolle

The Successful Speaker: Five Steps for Booking Gigs, Getting Paid, and Building Your Platform by Grant Baldwin with Jeff Goins

From Head to Toe by Eric Carle

Jemmy Button by Jennifer Uman and Valerio Vidali

Lolo's Sari-sari Store by Sophia N. Lee, illustrated by Christine Almeda

You Matter by Christian Robinson

No Matter What by Debi Gliori

Whistle for Willie by Ezra Jack Keats

Green Eggs and Ham by Dr. Seuss *(re-read)*

Just Me and My Dad by Mercer Mayer

One Love adapted by Cedella Marley, illustrated by Vanessa Brantley-Newton

We All Love: A Book for Compassionate Little Vegans and Vegetarians by Julie Hausen

Wacky Wednesday by Dr. Seuss writing as Theo. LeSieg, illustrated by George Booth

And Tango Makes Three by Justin Richardson and Peter Parnell, illustrated by Henry Cole

Llama Llama Jingle Bells by Anna Dewdney

Brown Bear, Brown Bear, What Do You See? by Bill Martin Jr., illustrated by Eric Carle

The Little Prince by Antoine de Saint-Exupéry

The Polar Express by Chris Van Allsburg

Sharing Is Caring by Brayden J. Renford and Bryan J. Renford, co-written by L. Marc Williams

The Alchemist by Paulo Coelho

The Moth Presents: A Point of Beauty: True Stories of Holding On and Letting Go edited by The Moth

Lighter: Let Go of the Past, Connect with the Present, and Expand the Future by Yung Pueblo

ABOUT THE AUTHOR

Oliver James is a California-based motivational speaker, literacy activist, and influencer. He has been featured on *Today*, *NPR*, *The Jennifer Hudson Show*, *Rachael Ray*, and *ABC News*, as well as in *Newsweek* and the *Los Angeles Times*. Additionally, he is the recent recipient of the 2023 Barbara Bush National Literacy Award. He lives in Costa Mesa, California.

Thank you for reading this book and for being a reader of books in general. We are so grateful to share being part of a community of readers with you, and we hope you will join us in passing our love of books on to the next generation of readers.

Did you know that reading for enjoyment is the single biggest predictor of a child's future happiness and success?

More than family circumstances, parents' educational background, or income, reading impacts a child's future academic performance, emotional well-being, communication skills, economic security, ambition, and happiness.

Studies show that kids reading for enjoyment in the US is in rapid decline:

- In 2012, 53% of 9-year-olds read almost every day. Just 10 years later, in 2022, the number had fallen to 39%.
- In 2012, 27% of 13-year-olds read for fun daily. By 2023, that number was just 14%.

Together, we can commit to **Raising Readers** and change this trend. How?

- Read to children in your life daily.
- Model reading as a fun activity.
- Reduce screen time.
- Start a family, school, or community book club.
- Visit bookstores and libraries regularly.
- Listen to audiobooks.
- Read the book before you see the movie.
- Encourage your child to read aloud to a pet or stuffed animal.
- Give books as gifts.
- Donate books to families and communities in need.

BOB1217

Books build bright futures, and **Raising Readers** is our shared responsibility.

For more information, visit **JoinRaisingReaders.com**

Sources: National Endowment for the Arts, National Assessment of Educational Progress, WorldBookDay.com, Nielsen BookData's 2023 "Understanding the Children's Book Consumer"

RAISING READERS